THE LITTLE BOOK OF BIG

MIND BENDERS

Over **450**

WORD PUZZLES,
NUMBER STUMPERS, RIDDLES,
BRAINTEASERS,
AND VISUAL CONUNDRUMS

SCOTT KIM

WORKMAN PUBLISHING · NEW YORK

Library of Congress Cataloging-in-Publication Data is available

ISBN 978-0-7611-7977-1

Design by Ariana Abud

PHOTO CREDITS: Adobe Natural Patterns (puzzles 1, 19, 73, 78,
83, 127, 132); Adobe Nifty Fifties (puzzle 24); Flicker Commons/Bennie
Nguyen (puzzle 199); istock.com (puzzles 42, 47, 91, 96, 101, 145, 150,
204, 209, 240, 245, 253, 263, 289, 299, 343, 348, 353, 366, 371, 397,
402, 407, 425); John and Karen Hollingsworth (puzzle 235); morguefile
.com (307, 317) sxc.hu (puzzles 253, 258, 312, 317, 415, 420); NASA
(puzzle 191); Wikimedia Commons (puzzles 6, 37, 47, 91, 137, 155, 181,
186, 199, 204, 209, 253, 258, 263, 307, 312, 317, 361, 366, 371, 415,
425).

Many of the puzzles in this collection have appeared previously
in *Discover, Games,* and *New Media* magazines, as well as the
Amazing Mind Benders calendar.

Workman books are available at special discounts when purchased in
bulk for premiums and sales promotions as well as for fund-raising or
educational use. Special editions or book excerpts also can be created to
specification. For details, contact the Special Sales Director at the address
below, or send an email to specialmarkets@workman.com.

Workman Publishing Company, Inc.
225 Varick Street
New York, NY 10014-4381

workman.com

WORKMAN is a registered trademark of Workman Publishing Co., Inc.

Printed in China
First printing July 2014

10 9 8 7 6 5 4 3 2 1

CONTENTS

INTRODUCTION

LIKE PUZZLES? KNOW SOMEONE WHO LIKES PUZZLES? You've come to the right place! You'll find oodles of them here, in this collection of over 450 of my favorite mind benders. I've included puzzles that exercise every part of your brain, from word and logic puzzles, to visual, number, and spatial puzzles. Some puzzles you'll recognize, like Word Search, Sudoku, and Mazes, while others will bend your mind, like Crazy Cross, in which letters read at more than one angle.

There are puzzles about garbled translation, classic movies, unfolded cubes, and shapes you can make with your hands. Every puzzle includes a hint, a difficulty rating (on a scale of one to four), and a place for you to check off each puzzle as you finish it.

Puzzles are color-coded by type: Look for green for visual puzzles, blue for logic, orange for number, pink for word, and teal for spatial. Puzzle types repeat every few pages, so keep an eye out for your favorites! And just to keep you on your toes, every so often there is a special medley of three related puzzles that don't appear anywhere else in the book.

Ever wonder where the ideas for puzzles come from? Here are the stories behind a few of the puzzles in this book. Go Figure (puzzle 13) is one of my favorite classic puzzles. You don't seem to have enough information to deduce the ages of three children. But you do. A real mind bender! This puzzle is pretty hard, so I made up a couple of easier puzzles (see puzzles 3 and 8) that lead up to it.

By Analogy (puzzle 30), Seek Whence (puzzle 115), and Speech Errors (puzzles 268–270) are drawn from the work of cognitive scientist Douglas Hofstadter, who thinks about they way we think. Hofstadter carries a notebook where he records overheard slips of the tongue, like a detective looking for evidence.

Body Shapes (puzzle 46) is drawn from the work I have done with teachers/performers Karl Schaffer and Erik Stern on classroom activities that are equal parts dance and mathematics. You can learn more at mathdance.org. I love using puzzles to inspire math students. Family Math (puzzles 70–72) presents three games from the Family Math program out of the Equals program at UC Berkeley.

I hope you enjoy this collection. If you have comments or questions, I'd love to hear from you.

Scott Kim, **scottkim.com**

PUZZLES

FIND where each detail appears in the big picture.

| 1 | 2 | 3 | 4 | 5 | 6 |

HINT: Detail 1 is in the upper middle.

FILL EACH GRID so every row, column, and colored region contains one of each number 1 to 6.

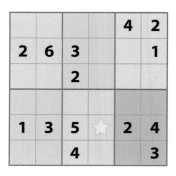

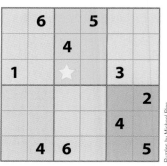

Puzzles by Michael Rios

HINT: Hint (Top): The star must be a 6 because every other number appears in the same row. Hint (Bottom): The star must be a 2 because every other number appears in the same row, column, or region.

3. GO FIGURE

IF YOU MULTIPLY the ages of my three kids, you get 24. The sum of their ages is 11. What are their three ages?

HINT: For instance, the ages 1, 2, and 12 multiply to 24 but add to 15.

4. OUT OF ORDER

UNSCRAMBLE the letters in each word pair to make two new words with opposite meanings, like "on vs. off."

TIDY HANG = _____ vs. _____

ONLY DOUG = _____ vs. _____

WRONG STEAK = _____ vs. _____

ISSUED EDITION = _____ vs. _____

HINT: time, age, power, location

HOW MANY squares of any size are in this grid?

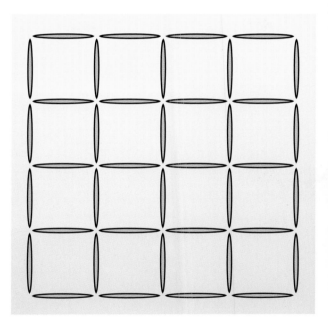

HINT: Squares come in four sizes.

WHAT COMMON THEME connects all three of these images? The answer may involve wordplay.

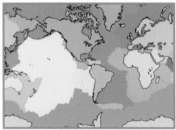

HINT: license, tectonic, dinner

HOW do the letters on the left differ from the letters on the right?

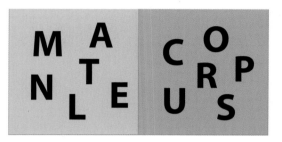

HINT: Try drawing the letters and seeing how your hand moves.

IF YOU MULTIPLY the ages of my three kids, you get 36. If you add their ages, what is the smallest possible sum you might get?

HINT: For instance, the three ages 1, 4, and 9 multiply to 36 and add to 14.

UNSCRAMBLE the letters in each word pair to make two new words with opposite meanings, like "on vs. off."

WELD ON = _____ vs. _____

FLUTE EARS = _____ vs. _____

EVER ROUND = _____ vs. _____

PROPOSES MILITIA = _____ vs. _____

HINT: preowned, veracity, altitude, equivalence

UNSCRAMBLE each set of nine tiles to spell the name of a famous written work. The two works are related. Do not rotate tiles.

WHICH TWO figures match perfectly?

1. 2. 3. 4.

5. 6. 7. 8.

HINT: Neither figure 1 nor figure 4 is part of the perfect match.

ABE AND BARB sat as far away from each other as possible. Carl and Deb sat next to each other. Ed sat in the red chair. Where did Fay sit?

HINT: Abe and Barb must have sat in either seats 1 and 6, or in seats 2 and 5.

13. GO FIGURE

IF YOU MULTIPLY the ages of my three kids, you get 36. If I tell you the sum of their ages, you cannot deduce all the ages with certainty. But if I also add that the oldest kid is at least a year older than the other kids, you could then deduce all the ages. What are their three ages?

HINT: There must be two sets of ages that add to that particular sum.

OUT OF ORDER

UNSCRAMBLE the letters in each word pair to make two new words with opposite meanings, like "on vs. off."

FOLD OUTS = _____ vs. _____

HEAD RAYS = _____ vs. _____

BLEAK WITCH = _____ vs. _____

BOXER KNIFED = _____ vs. _____

HINT: decibels, difficulty, brightness, repair status

WHICH TWO patterns look the same when folded into cubes?

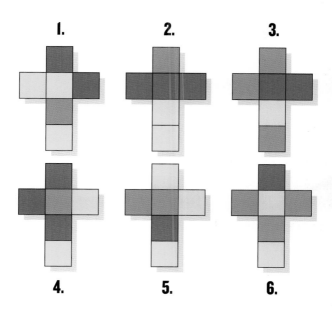

HINT: Pattern 1 is not one of the two matching patterns.

THE WORD TATTOO, when written as a stack of capital letters, has a vertical axis of symmetry. Fill in the blanks with other words that have the same mirror symmetry. For instance, the first word is ATOM. The first letters of the words, reading down, spell a word meaning "vending machine."

1. ☐ _ _ _ _ Small particle
2. ☐ _ _ _ _ Salt Lake state
3. ☐ _ _ Plaything
4. ☐ _ _ _ _ _ _ To get the better of
5. ☐ _ _ _ _ Legendary story
6. ☐ _ _ _ Opposite of toward
7. ☐ _ _ _ _ _ Vine-ripened fruit

HINT: The first three words start with the letters A, U, and T.

THE WORD ICEBOX, when written in capital letters, has a horizontal axis of symmetry. Fill in the blanks with other words that have the same mirror symmetry. For instance, the first word is DODO. The first letters of the words, reading down, spell a word meaning "translated into ordinary language."

1. ☐ _ _ _ Extinct bird
2. ☐ _ _ _ Sonic reflection
3. ☐ _ _ _ _ Verify
4. ☐ _ _ _ Woodwind instrument   -ICEBOX-
5. ☐ _ _ _ _ _ To make a judgment
6. ☐ _ _ _ _ What the tide did
7. ☐ _ _ _ _ _ _ Carbon molecule you exhale

HINT: The first three words start with the letters D, E, and C.

PUZZLE TYPE: SPATIAL
COMPLETION: ☐

DIFFICULTY: ✿✿✿
TIME: _____

THE STARTING POSITION below shows a stack of three blocks, weighing 1, 3, and 9 pounds. How they fall depends on which block weighs which amount. The small diagrams show the same blocks one second later. Label the blocks in each diagram with the correct weights.
Diagram 1 is already labeled.

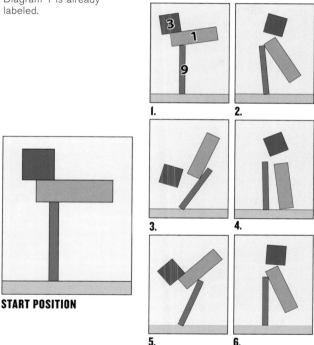

START POSITION

1.   2.   3.   4.   5.   6.

HINT: If the yellow block is heavier than the red block, both blocks fall to the right.

FIND where each detail appears in the big picture.

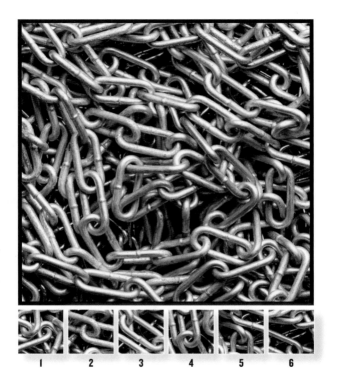

| 1 | 2 | 3 | 4 | 5 | 6 |

HINT: Detail 1 is in the lower right.

PUT the letters in the boxes so every row and column spells a common word.

BEN is five years older than his brother Alex. In three years Ben will be twice Alex's age. What are their two ages now?

THESE WELL-KNOWN SAYINGS were translated by a computer to another language, then back into English, with surprising results. What were the original sayings?

> Hush it is gilded.
>
> It observes before that you jump.
>
> All land transportations cause Rome.
>
> A strong box better than grieved.
>
> Any rise must get down.

HINT: Think literally. What is a four-letter word for "strong box"?

START at one of the orange rooms, go through doorways to visit every room just once, and end in the other orange room. You must alternate passing through red and purple walls. Start with either color.

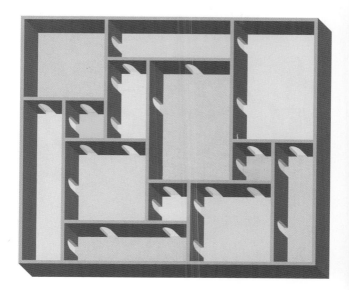

FIND where each detail appears in the big picture.

| I | 2 | 3 | 4 | 5 | 6 |

HINT: Detail 1 is in the mouth.

25. CATEGORIES

HOW do the figures on the left differ from the figures on the right?

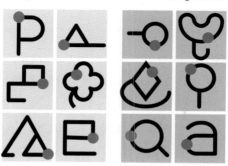

HINT: What's under the dot?

26. GO FIGURE

BEN is three times the age of his brother Alex. In three years Ben will be twice Alex's age. What are their two ages now?

HINT: Both brothers are younger than 20.

FIND 19 words of four or more letters, spelled forward or backward, straight or diagonal, that combine with PAPER to make a common word or phrase. The leftover letters spell a relevant quotation.

```
T A V R E R B C A L C C
O H W H I T E O L H N C
T N G T R C A N A L I C
C I A I I T E S I G A S
U K I R E S E T A N T W
T P R W E W S R N E W S
T A P O R G E U T H T H
E N L E Y T I C E P C M
R A A E T P E T W R L A
I T N E T E L I O T I C
S O E D N A S O R W P H
M R I T T E N N K O N E
```

HINT: The second word of the quotation is "verbal."

WHICH SHAPES can be made by assembling the two pieces at right?

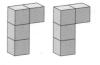

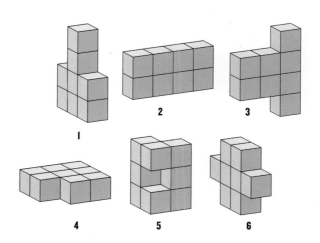

1

2

3

4

5

6

HINT: Of the six shapes given, there are two that cannot be assembled.

FIND where each detail appears in the big picture.

1   2   3   4   5   6

HINT: Details are enlarged 200%. Detail 1 is in the top left.

PUZZLE TYPE: LOGIC	DIFFICULTY: ✸
COMPLETION: ☐	TIME: _____

AT RIGHT are the first four letters of four different "grid fonts." Draw each missing "e" in the style of the other letters in the same font. The first "e" is in place. There may be more than one "e" shape for some fonts.

HINT: What is the shape theme of each font?

PUZZLE TYPE: NUMBER	DIFFICULTY: ✸✸✸
COMPLETION: ☐	TIME: _____

BEN is older than his brother Alex. In three years adding their ages will give you the same number as multiplying their ages today. What are their two ages now?

HINT: Both brothers are younger than 20.

| PUZZLE TYPE: WORD | DIFFICULTY: ✿ |
| COMPLETION: ☐ | TIME: _____ |

FILL IN the missing words to turn CAT into DOG. Each word differs from the previous word in just one letter, like this: THIS–THIN–THAN–THAT. There are two solutions for the second missing word. Can you find them both?

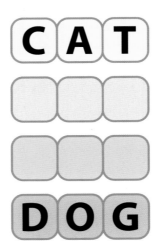

HINT: Change the A in CAT to O.

LAY SIX SHEETS of stationery flat on a table so each sheet touches exactly two other sheets. Sheets may overlap but may not be folded, cut, or bent.

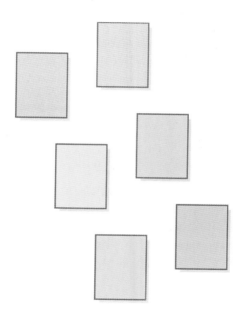

HINT: There are two different solutions.

34. THE 15 PUZZLE A

| PUZZLE TYPE: LOGIC
| COMPLETION: ☐

DIFFICULTY: ✿ ✿ ✿
TIME: _____

LONG BEFORE SUDOKU, another number puzzle called the 15 Puzzle took the world by storm. You are given 15 wooden blocks in a square frame, numbered 1 to 15, with the last two blocks, 15 and 14, out of order. Your goal is to slide the blocks back into order without taking them out of the frame. The standard 15 Puzzle with square blocks has no solution, but this version with round blocks does. What's the trick?

START POSITION

END POSITION (solved)

Photos by Jerry Slocum

IT TURNS OUT that the 15 Puzzle is impossible to solve, a fact that the puzzlemaker knew but failed to tell purchasers. To get a feeling for why a sliding block puzzle can be impossible to solve, explain why it is impossible to slide the blocks in the puzzle shown below at left to make the configuration of blocks shown below at right.

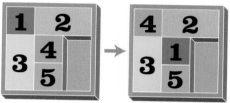

HINT: Focus on blocks 1, 2, and 3.

EXPLAIN WHY it is impossible to slide the blocks in the puzzle shown below at left to make the configuration of blocks shown below at right.

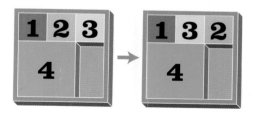

HINT: Pretend block 4 is the earth, and blocks 1, 2, and 3 are the moons.

| PUZZLE TYPE: VISUAL | DIFFICULTY: ✿✿ |
| COMPLETION: ☐ | TIME: _____ |

WHAT COMMON THEME connects all three of these images? The answer may involve wordplay.

HINT: count

FILL EACH GRID so every row, column, and colored region contains one of each number 1 to 6. The marked diagonals must also contain one of each number 1 to 6.

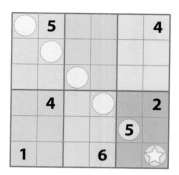

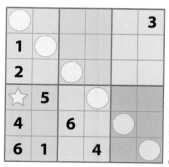

Puzzles by Michael Rios

ADA AND BETH met at a party. "I'm 24," said Ada. "That's curious," said Beth. "All of my kids have ages that divide evenly into your age." If no two kids are the same age, what is the most number of kids Beth could have?

HINT: Beth has between 4 and 10 kids.

THESE TITLES of classic movies were translated by a computer to another language, then back into English, with surprising results. What were the original titles?

ASTERISK WARS (1977)

POSTERIOR WINDOW (1954)

IT OCCURRED DURING A NIGHT (1934)

CONJECTURE THAT IS COMING TO THE LUNCH (1967)

HINT: Mark, Jimmy, Clark, Sidney

PUZZLE TYPE: SPATIAL
COMPLETION: ☐

DIFFICULTY: ✿✿✿
TIME: _____

MATCH EACH DETAIL with a different letter. For instance, detail 1 is from the A. All details are right side up and magnified the same amount.

DINOSAUR
___ ___ ___ ___ ___ ___₁ ___ ___

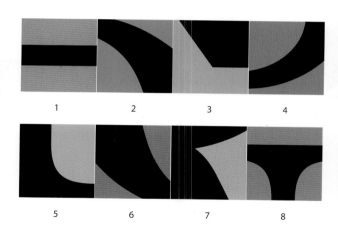

1   2   3   4

5   6   7   8

HINT: Detail 2 is from the D.

WHAT COMMON THEME connects all three of these images? The answer may involve wordplay.

HINT: rhyme time

43. SEEK WHENCE

PUZZLE TYPE: LOGIC
COMPLETION: ☐
DIFFICULTY: ✲✲
TIME: ______

EXPLAIN why the sequence

1 1 2 1 1 2...

could be logically continued as any of the following:

A ...3 1 1 2 3 4 1 1

B ...3 2 1 1 2 3 4 3

C ...1 1 2 1 1 2 1 1

For instance, the sequence **1 2 1 2 3**
could be continued as the expanding sequence
(1 2) (1 2 3) (1 2 3 4) (1 2 3 4 5) . . .
or as the paired sequence
(1 2) (1 2) (3 4) (3 4) (5 6) (5 6) . . .

HINT: Group the first sequence as (1 1 2) (1 1 2 3) (1 1 2 3 4) (1 1).

I HAVE THREE KIDS, all of different ages. No number except 1 divides evenly into all their ages, but for each pair of kids there is a unique number bigger than 1 that divides evenly into both ages. No kid is older than 20. What are their three ages?

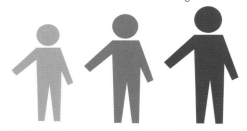

HINT: For instance, the numbers 2 and 4 both divide evenly into the ages 4 and 12, so 4 and 12 cannot be two of the ages.

DECODE these two familiar terms.

HINT: almost at the finish line; quaint yarn

| PUZZLE TYPE: SPATIAL | DIFFICULTY: ☀ |
| COMPLETION: ☐ | TIME: _____ |

FOUR PEOPLE are making an octagon by holding one another's wrists. Instead of one octagon, how can they make two squares by holding wrists? Can they make two polygons with different numbers of sides?

Photo by Steve Dibartolomeo

HINT: One solution is to start by joining right hands to make a square.

WHAT COMMON THEME connects all three of these images? The answer may involve wordplay.

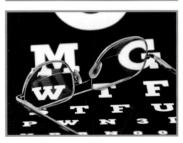

HINT: founding father

EACH LETTER in the sum stands for a different digit. For instance, E equals 5. Can you find the values of the other letters? If a letter appears more than once, it always stands for the same digit. The first digit of a number is never 0. Use logic to deduce digits: Why must S equal 1?

HINT: S must equal 1; it is a carryover from the ten thousands place. V equals 3.

49. GO FIGURE

BOB'S KIDS are all at least 10 years old and no more than 20. There is no number bigger than 1 that divides evenly into two of the kids' ages. What is the most number of kids Bob could have?

HINT: The ages cannot include both 12 and 18 because 6 divides both.

50. SECRET WORD

DEDUCE the secret five-letter word from the clues. For instance, the word WRITE shares three letter tiles with the word RIGHT.

The secret word

shares four tiles with

C A K E D

and shares four tiles with

C H I D E

HINT: The secret word starts with the letter A.

HOW MANY circular holes are here?

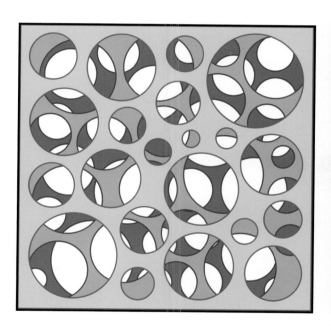

HINT: Count the holes in each layer separately.

THE POPULAR electronic game Tetris was created by Russian mathematician Alexey Pajitnov in 1985. In this Tetris board, your goal is to rotate the L shape at top, then slide it down, left and right (not up) until it lands on another piece or stops at the bottom of the "well." The other pieces do not move. How many landing positions are possible? Two are shown.

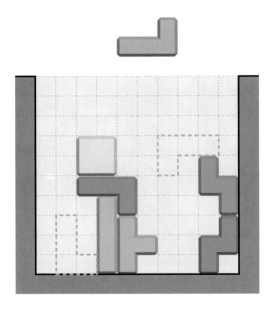

HINT: Consider all four rotations. Legal landing positions can appear unbalanced.

DROP the seven pieces in the given order to fill the well. When you drop a piece, rotate it, then slide it down, left, and right (not up) until it lands on another. The other pieces do not move. You may not slide a piece through another. The solution is unique.

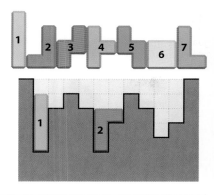

HINT: Drop piece 3 into the bottom of the rightmost canyon.

DROP the seven pieces in the given order to fill the well. When you drop a piece, rotate it, then slide it down, left, and right (not up) until it lands on another. The other pieces do not move. You may not slide a piece through another. The solution is unique.

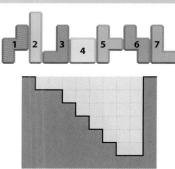

HINT: Pieces 1 and 2 touch the right edge of the well; piece 3 touches the left edge.

WHICH TWO figures match perfectly? Figures may be rotated.

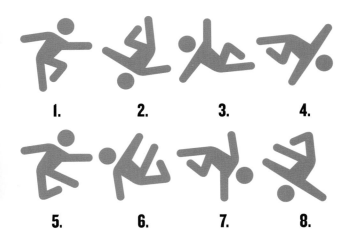

1.   **2.**   **3.**   **4.**

5.   **6.**   **7.**   **8.**

HINT: Neither figure 4 nor figure 5 is part of the perfect match.

PUT the numbers in the boxes so every row, column, and main diagonal adds up to the same number.

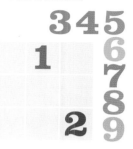

HINT: The center number is 5.

ZANE IS OLDER than Mabel, and both have two-digit ages. Zane's age is the same as Mabel's age backward, and Mabel's age doubled is within a year of Zane's age. How old is Zane?

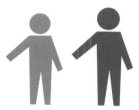

HINT: For instance, if Zane is 21, then Mabel is 12.

PUZZLE TYPE: WORD	DIFFICULTY: ✹
COMPLETION: ▢	TIME: _____

IN THIS CROSSWORD each letter reads in two directions. Copy letters from the alphabet at top into the empty boxes. You may rotate and flip letters. Each word reads in the direction of its clue. The first letter is given.

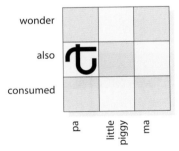

wonder

also

consumed

pa

little piggy

ma

UNSCRAMBLE each set of nine tiles to spell the name of a famous written work. The two works are related. Do not rotate tiles.

HINT: Both works were written by Homer.

WHICH TWO figures match perfectly?

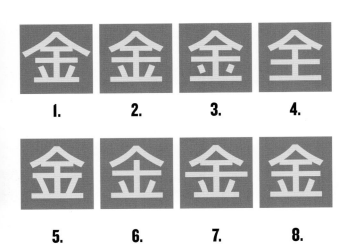

1.   2.   3.   4.

5.   6.   7.   8.

HINT: Neither figure 4 nor figure 5 is part of the perfect match.

PUZZLE TYPE: LOGIC
COMPLETION: ☐

DIFFICULTY: ✿✿
TIME: _____

HOW do the figures on the left differ from the figures on the right?

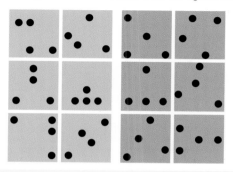

HINT: You're getting closer.

62. GO FIGURE

PUZZLE TYPE: NUMBER
COMPLETION: ☐

DIFFICULTY: ✿✿✿✿
TIME: _____

ZANE is at least a year older than Mabel, and both are less then 10 years old. If you write their ages side by side, you get a single number. If you write their ages side by side in the same order in 30 months you will get a number exactly three times as large. How old is Zane?

HINT: Mabel is 1 year old.

FIND 19 words of four or more letters, spelled forward or backward, straight or diagonal, that combine with FREE to make a common word or phrase. The leftover letters spell a relevant quotation.

R	G	F	N	R	E	E	F	O	R	M	D
A	O	N	O	G	N	I	K	N	I	H	T
G	T	M	I	E	R	O	F	T	H	N	E
U	Y	R	T	T	C	A	P	R	O	E	G
S	R	S	A	S	A	N	D	S	I	N	S
S	I	A	I	D	L	O	A	I	I	I	M
E	A	G	C	I	E	M	L	L	C	R	T
R	D	E	O	E	D	L	E	F	E	A	F
P	N	N	S	T	O	E	L	D	T	A	L
H	A	T	S	O	H	S	A	I	L	E	W
H	H	O	A	W	O	O	W	L	W	N	O
N	H	C	N	U	L	E	L	Y	T	S	E

HINT: The longest hidden word is "association."

WHICH TWO patterns look the same when folded into cubes?

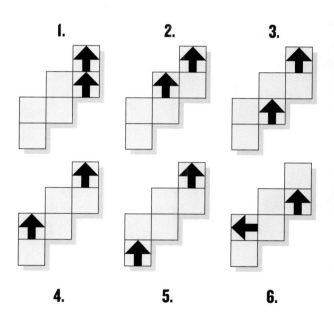

I. **2.** **3.**

4. **5.** **6.**

HINT: Pattern 6 is not one of the two matching patterns.

WHICH TWO figures match perfectly? Figures may be rotated.

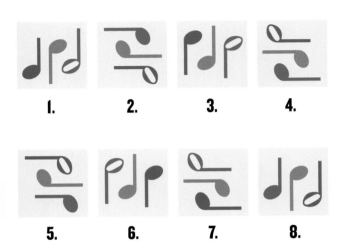

1.   2.   3.   4.

5.   6.   7.   8.

HINT: Neither figure 7 nor figure 3 is part of the perfect match.

| PUZZLE TYPE: LOGIC | DIFFICULTY: ☀ |
| COMPLETION: ☐ | TIME: _____ |

EACH EQUATION below uses the same rule to combine letters of two words to make a third word. Figure out the rule, then fill in the missing word.

SEAT + AGAR = STAR

GAIN + ABET = GNAT

FOUR + ELSE = FREE

LOGO + CALK =

HINT: alpha and omega

| PUZZLE TYPE: NUMBER | DIFFICULTY: ☀☀ |
| COMPLETION: ☐ | TIME: _____ |

ZANE is at least a year older than Mabel, and both are at least 10 years old. If you write their ages on a calculator, one age is the same as the other age turned upside down. If the difference between their ages is as small as possible, how old is Zane?

HINT: For instance, 18 is the same as 81 turned upside down.

FILL IN the missing words to turn LOGS into FIRE. Each word differs from the previous word in just one letter, like this: THIS–THIN–THAN–THAT. There are two completely different solutions. Can you find them both?

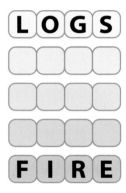

L O G S

☐☐☐☐

☐☐☐☐

☐☐☐☐

F I R E

HINT: Change either the first or last letter of LOGS.

JOIN the matching numbered circles by drawing paths that follow edges. Paths may not collide, but they can pass in front of each other on different layers. One path is already drawn. Note: There is more than one solution.

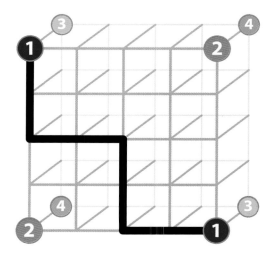

HINT: Paths 1 and 4 are the same shape, as are paths 2 and 3.

70. FAMILY MATH A

THIS IS A GAME for two people. Lay 10 pennies on a table. Players take turns removing one or two pennies at a time. Players may not skip turns. The player who takes the last penny wins. Which player can always win—player 1 or player 2—and what is the winning strategy?

HINT: First play the game with three pennies. Once you have found the winning strategy, move on to six pennies. Then keep adding pennies.

71. FAMILY MATH B

IN THE DIAGRAM below, four pieces of straight dried spaghetti, all the same length, cross one another at six points. That's the most number of crossings you can get with four pieces of spaghetti. What is the most number of crossings you can get with five pieces of straight dried spaghetti? With six pieces? Seven pieces? Eight? What's the pattern?

HINT: How many times can two straight pieces of spaghetti cross each other?

SELECT ten cards (ace, 2, 3, and so on up to 10) from a deck. Make a stack of cards by placing the 10 facedown on the table, followed by the 9 facedown on top of that, followed by the 8 facedown on top of that, and so on until you place the ace facedown on top of the stack last. Now we're going to make a new stack by alternating between two actions: First, turn over the top card of the old stack, which will be the ace, and place it faceup on the table to start a new stack. Then move the top card of your old stack to the bottom of the old stack, keeping it facedown. Keep repeating: Move the top card onto the new stack faceup, then move the top card to the bottom of the old stack facedown. Keep going until there is just one card left in the old stack; place that card faceup on the new stack. Can you predict the order of the card in the new stack without actually touching the cards?

| A | 2 | 3 | 4 | 5 | 6 | 7 | 8 | 9 | 10 |

HINT: To predict the order without actually touching the cards, start by writing A, 1, 2, 3, . . . 10 in a circle.

PUZZLE TYPE: VISUAL	DIFFICULTY: ✹ ✹
COMPLETION: ☐	TIME: _____

FIND where each detail appears in the big picture.

| 1 | 2 | 3 | 4 | 5 | 6 |

HINT: Detail 1 is above middle.

FILL EACH GRID so every row, column, and colored region contains one of each number 1 to 6. The marked diagonals must also contain one of each number 1 to 6.

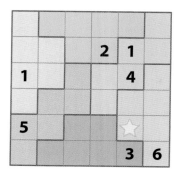

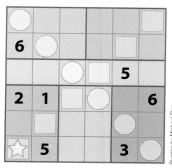

Puzzles by Michael Rios

HINT: In the top puzzle, the star must be a 2 because every other number appears in the same row, column, or region. In the bottom puzzle, the star must be a 4 because every other number appears in the same row, column, or region.

HERE are two different ways to fit five pieces into a black box. What is the total number of ways to fit these five pieces into the box?

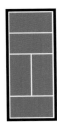 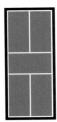

HINT: Each piece is two squares long. Vertical pieces appear in pairs that form squares.

UNSCRAMBLE the letters in each word pair to make two new words with opposite meanings, like "on vs. off."

AIR TOWEL = _____ vs. _____

REALLY EAT = _____ vs. _____

UPSTATE FUR = _____ vs. _____

NIFTY IONIZER = _____ vs. _____

HINT: don't mix, gets the worm, time, quantity

WHICH SHAPES below can be made by cutting the shape at right into two pieces and reassembling?

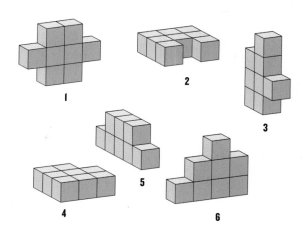

1

2

3

4

5

6

HINT: Of the six shapes given, there are two that cannot be assembled.

THE LITTLE BOOK OF BIG MIND BENDERS   **61**

PUZZLE TYPE: VISUAL	DIFFICULTY: ✿✿
COMPLETION: ☐	TIME: _____

FIND where each detail appears in the big picture.

| 1 | 2 | 3 | 4 | 5 | 6 |

HINT: Detail 1 is right of middle.

HOW do the letters on the left differ from the letters on the right?

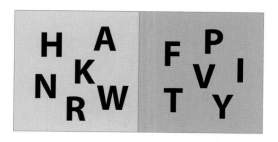

HINT: Imagine the letters are sculptures 20 feet tall and you are walking among them.

HERE are two different ways to fit six pieces into a black box. What is the total number of ways to fit these six pieces into the box?

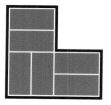 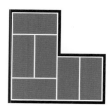

HINT: Each piece is two squares long. Every solution has 0, 2, 4, or 6 vertical pieces.

| PUZZLE TYPE: WORD | DIFFICULTY: ✹✹ |
| COMPLETION: ☐ | TIME: _____ |

DECODE these two familiar phrases.

HINT: cosmic concepts

PUZZLE TYPE: SPATIAL	DIFFICULTY: ✿✿
COMPLETION: ☐	TIME: _____

LAY SIX SHEETS of stationery flat on a table so each sheet touches exactly three other sheets. Sheets may overlap, but may not be folded, cut, or bent. At most, three sheets may touch at one corner.

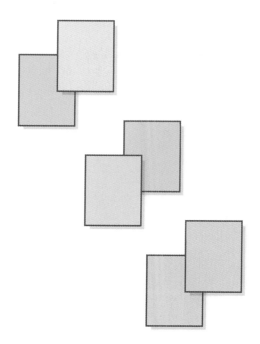

HINT: Arrange the sheets in two layers of three sheets each.

FIND where each detail appears in the big picture.

| 1 | 2 | 3 | 4 | 5 | 6 |

HINT: Detail 1 is in upper left.

ABE AND BARB sat as far away from each other as possible. Carl sat behind and one seat to the left of Deb. Ed sat farther to the right than Deb. Where did Fay sit?

HINT: Abe and Barb must have sat in either seats 1 and 6, or in seats 3 and 4.

85. ASSEMBLIES

PUZZLE TYPE: NUMBER	DIFFICULTY: ✿✿
COMPLETION: ☐	TIME: _____

HERE are two different ways to fit six pieces into a black box. What is the total number of ways to fit these six pieces into the box?

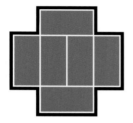 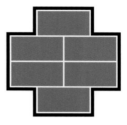

HINT: Each piece is two squares long. Every solution has 2 squares made of 2 pieces.

86. SECRET WORD

PUZZLE TYPE: WORD	DIFFICULTY: ✿✿
COMPLETION: ☐	TIME: _____

DEDUCE the secret five-letter word from the clues. For instance, the word WRITE shares three letter tiles with the word RIGHT.

The secret word

☐ ☐ ☐ ☐ ☐

shares three tiles with

J U I C E

and shares four tiles with

T A U P E

HINT: The secret word starts with the letter A.

MATCH EACH DETAIL with a different letter. For instance, detail 6 is from the T. All details are right side up and magnified the same amount.

triangles

6 ___ ___ ___ ___ ___ ___ ___ ___

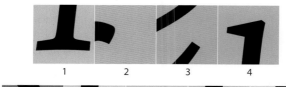

1   2   3   4

5   6   7   8   9

HINT: Detail 1 is from the L.

| PUZZLE TYPE: SPATIAL | DIFFICULTY: ☀ |
| COMPLETION: ☐ | TIME: _____ |

INVENTED more than 200 years ago, the seven Tangram shapes join to make a square and myriad other shapes. Find each figure below outlined in the grid of nine Tangram squares. Each outlined figure contains every Tangram shape once. Only one answer is given.

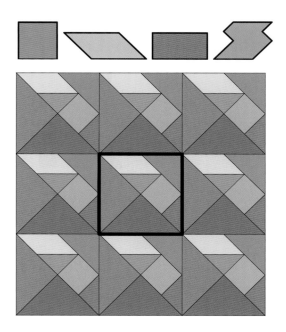

HINT: The square is given. All other shapes appear rotated.

PUZZLE TYPE: SPATIAL	DIFFICULTY: ✹
COMPLETION: ☐	TIME: _____

FIND each figure below outlined in the grid of nine Tangram squares at right. Each figure contains all seven Tangram shapes once. One answer is given.

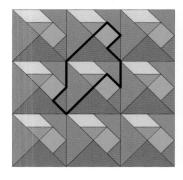

HINT: All figures are rotated at a diagonal angle.

PUZZLE TYPE: SPATIAL	DIFFICULTY: ✹✹
COMPLETION: ☐	TIME: _____

FIND each figure below outlined in the grid of nine Tangram squares at right. Each figure contains all seven Tangram shapes once. One answer is given.

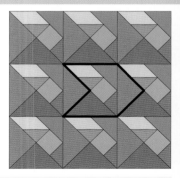

HINT: The first and last figures are not rotated. The others are rotated by 45 degrees.

WHAT COMMON THEME connects all three of these images? The answer may involve wordplay.

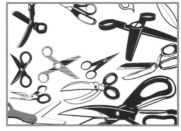

HINT: The other hand.

PUT the letters in the boxes so every row and column spells a common word.

HERE are two different ways to fit five pieces into a black box. What is the total number of ways to fit these five pieces into the box?

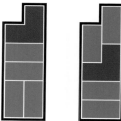

THESE WELL-KNOWN SAYINGS were translated by a computer to another language, then back into English, with surprising results. What were the original sayings?

> Trade in front of pleasure.
>
> The love is without visibility.
>
> Because of your sow, therefore you will harvest.
>
> Many chefs damage the soup.
>
> Let the customers watch out.

HINT: What is a five-letter word for "without visibility"?

FOUR PEOPLE extend the thumb, index finger, and middle finger of each hand. How can they join their fingers together to make a cube?

Photo by Steve Dibartolomeo

HINT: Everyone start by joining their own two thumbs together to make a straight edge.

WHAT COMMON THEME connects all three of these images? The answer may involve wordplay.

HINT: 100 shares of what?

HOW do the figures on the left differ from the figures on the right?

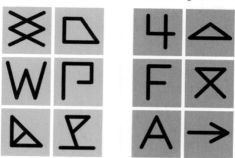

HERE are two different ways to fit four pieces into a black box. What is the total number of ways to fit these four pieces into the box?

PUZZLE TYPE: WORD
COMPLETION: ☐

DIFFICULTY: ✿ ✿
TIME: _____

FIND 20 words of four or more letters, spelled forward or backward, straight or diagonal, that combine with WELL to make a common word or phrase, such as WELLHOUSE, which means a house built over a well or source of water. The leftover letters spell a relevant quotation.

T	B	R	E	D	G	N	I	E	B	G	D
H	G	E	N	E	K	O	P	S	N	E	R
E	N	W	O	N	K	W	A	I	D	R	D
O	I	F	A	I	T	H	R	N	I	D	G
I	H	N	G	F	W	P	U	N	E	N	E
L	S	L	D	E	S	O	F	V	I	D	A
D	I	O	E	D	R	O	R	N	E	D	D
N	W	E	S	E	R	E	A	D	E	E	V
I	N	S	S	M	S	E	N	L	L	T	I
O	R	H	E	E	M	U	E	I	A	V	S
E	O	D	R	D	O	E	O	F	A	R	E
O	W	P	D	F	H	N	E	H	I	T	D

HINT: One of the hidden words is "preserved."

HOW MANY times does this shape appear in the figure below, at any size or angle? Mirror images are allowed. Shown below is one occurrence.

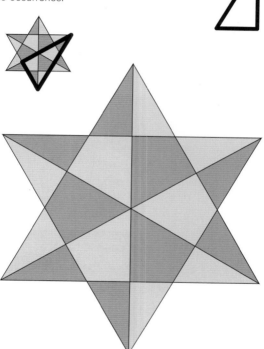

HINT: The shape appears in three sizes.

WHAT COMMON THEME connects all three of these images? The answer may involve wordplay.

HINT: two by two

EACH EQUATION below uses the same rule to combine letters of two words to make a third word. Figure out the rule, then fill in the missing word.

$$\text{SEAT} + \text{AGAR} = \text{STAR}$$

$$\text{OVER} + \text{ERAS} = \text{ORES}$$

$$\text{LOSE} + \text{ALAS} = \text{LESS}$$

$$\text{PAIR} + \text{TEAM} =$$

HINT: Which A?

HERE are two different ways to fit four pieces into a black box. What is the total number of ways to fit these four pieces into the box?

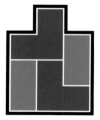 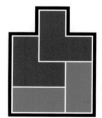

HINT: First place the purple pieces, then place the green pieces.

FILL IN the missing words to turn GAIN into LOSS. Each word differs from the previous word in just one letter, like this: THIS– THIN–THAN–THAT.

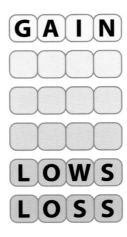

UNSCRAMBLE each set of nine tiles to spell the name of a famous written work. The two works are related. Do not rotate tiles.

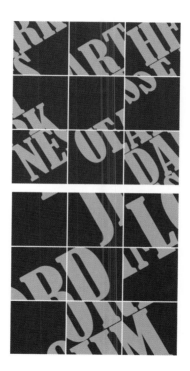

HINT: Both works were written by Joseph Conrad.

IN THIS MAGIC WORD SQUARE, every square contains a different two-letter word (some of which are uncommon), and every row and column contains the letters of the name ADONIS. Can you fill in the missing words?

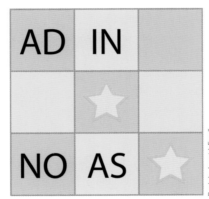

Puzzle by Jeremiah Farrell

HINT: Start by filling in the starred squares. For instance, the middle square contains DO.

IN THIS MAGIC WORD SQUARE,
every square contains a different two-letter word (some of which are uncommon), and every row, column, and main diagonal contains the letters of the word ASTEROID. Can you fill in the missing words?

Puzzle by Jeremiah Farrell

HINT: Start by filling in the starred squares. For instance, the upper right square must contain TO because all other letters already appear in the same row or column.

IN THIS MAGIC WORD SQUARE,
every square contains a different two-letter word (some of which are uncommon) and every row, column, and main diagonal contains the letters of the word MOUSTERIAN. Can you fill in the missing words?

Puzzle by Jeremiah Farrell

HINT: Start by filling in the starred squares. For instance, the middle square contains the word AS. "Mousterian" is the name archaeologists use for stone age flint hand tools.

WHICH TWO figures match perfectly? Figures may not be rotated.

1.

2.

3.

4.

5.

6.

7.

8.

HINT: The two matching figures do not include figure 1 or figure 2.

FILL EACH GRID so every row, column, and colored region contains one of each number 1 to 6. The marked diagonals must also contain one of each number 1 to 6.

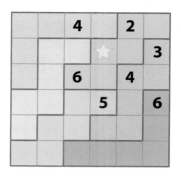

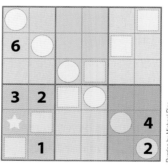

Puzzles by Michael Rios

HINT: In the top puzzle, the star must be a 4 because that is the only empty square in the green region that is not in the same row or column as another 4. In the bottom puzzle, the star must be a 5 because every other number appears in the same row, column, or region.

THE LITTLE BOOK OF **BIG MIND BENDERS** **87**

HERE are are two different ways to fit four pieces into a black box. What is the total number of ways to fit these four pieces into the box?

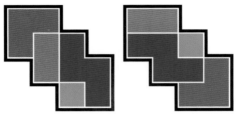

HINT: First place the dark blue piece. Then fit the other smaller pieces around it.

THESE TITLES of classic movies were translated by a computer to another language, then back into English, with surprising results. What were the original titles?

SIMPLE PASSENGER (1969)

ON THE EDGE OF SEA (1954)

REVOLTING ON THE PREMIUM (1935)

ALL ALLEVIATE ON WESTERN FACE (1930)

HINT: Fonda, Brando, Gable, Ayres

WHICH TWO patterns look the same when folded into cubes?

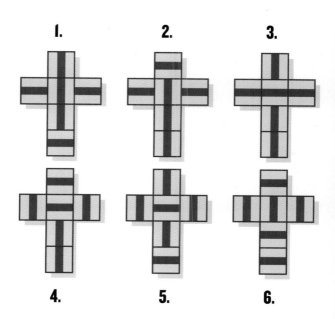

1. **2.** **3.**

4. **5.** **6.**

HINT: Pattern 6 is not one of the two matching patterns.

WHICH TWO figures match perfectly? Figures may be rotated.

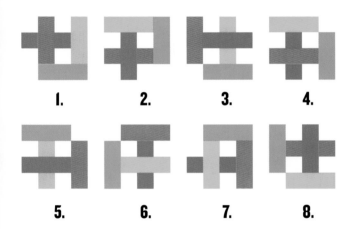

1.   **2.**   **3.**   **4.**

5.   **6.**   **7.**   **8.**

HINT: The two matching figures do not include figure 7 or figure 8.

115. SEEK WHENCE

PUZZLE TYPE: LOGIC
COMPLETION: ☐

DIFFICULTY: ✲✲
TIME: ________

EXPLAIN why the sequence

1 0 0 1 1 1...

could be logically continued as any of the following:

A ...0 0 0 0 1 1 1 1

B ...1 1 1 2 2 1 1 3

C ...1 2 2 1 3 3 1 4

For instance, the sequence **1 2 1 2 3**
could be continued as the expanding sequence
(1 2) (1 2 3) (1 2 3 4) (1 2 3 4 5) . . .
or as the paired sequence
(1 2) (1 2) (3 4) (3 4) (5 6) (5 6) . . .

HINT: Group the second sequence as (1 0 0 1) (1 1 1 1) (1 2 2 1) (1 3 . . .

HERE ARE two different ways to fit four pieces into a black box. What is the total number of ways to fit these four pieces into the box?

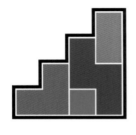

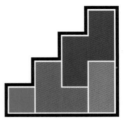

HINT: First place the dark blue piece, then fit the other smaller pieces around it.

DECODE these two related familiar phrases.

GNIREENIGNE

ELBITAPMOC

HINT: hardware and software

START in room 4 and visit every room just once. You must alternate bigger and smaller numbers. For instance, if you go from room 5 to room 6, you must then go to the smaller number 2, not 8 or 11.

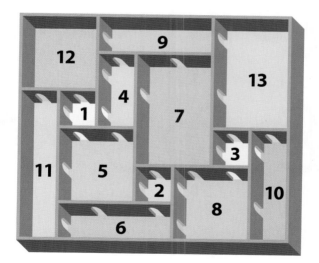

HINT: Start in room 4 and end in room 8.

WHICH TWO figures match perfectly? Figures may not be rotated.

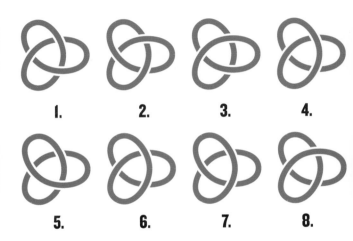

1.

2.

3.

4.

5.

6.

7.

8.

HINT: The two matching figures do not include figure 1 or figure 2.

EACH LETTER in the sum stands for a different digit. For instance, E equals 7. Can you find the values of the other letters? If a letter appears more than once, it always stands for the same digit. The first digit of a number is never 0. Use logic to deduce digits: Why must H equal 9?

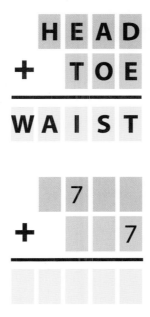

HINT: H must equal 9 because H plus the carryover from the hundreds place equals 10. T equals 5.

121. ASSEMBLIES

| PUZZLE TYPE: NUMBER | DIFFICULTY: ✿✿✿ |
| COMPLETION: ☐ | TIME: _____ |

HERE are two different ways to fit four pieces into a black box. What is the total number of ways to fit these four pieces into the box?

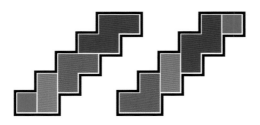

HINT: First place the dark blue piece at left, then fit the other smaller pieces to the right.

122. SECRET WORD

| PUZZLE TYPE: WORD | DIFFICULTY: ✿✿✿ |
| COMPLETION: ☐ | TIME: _____ |

DEDUCE the secret five-letter word from the clues. For instance, the word WRITE shares three letter tiles with the word RIGHT.

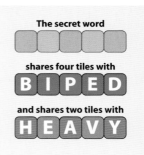

The secret word

☐ ☐ ☐ ☐ ☐

shares four tiles with

B I P E D

and shares two tiles with

H E A V Y

HINT: The secret word starts with the letter A.

WHICH SHAPES can be made by
assembling the two pieces at right?
Some cubes may be hidden.

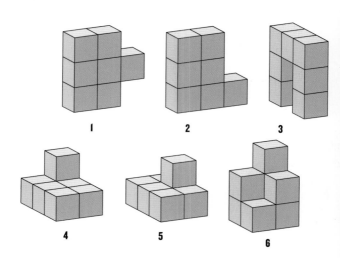

1

2

3

4

5

6

HINT: Of the six shapes given, there are two that cannot be assembled.

THE FASCINATING PROGRAM *The Geometer's Sketchpad* from Key Curriculum Press (keypress.com) lets students construct dynamic figures that roll, hinge, and leave traces when parts are moved. In the figure below a wheel rolls to the right. The blue point travels in a straight line. What paths do the purple and red points trace?

A CIRCLE ROLLS around the inside of a circle twice its size. The blue middle point travels in a circle. What paths do the purple and red points follow?

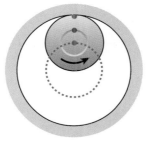

HINT: The path of the red dot is surprisingly simple.

THREE BARS pivot at four points. The black points are attached firmly to the ground. As the blue point traces the circle, what paths do the purple and red points trace? Note: Bars never collide with one another, even if it appears that they might.

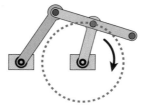

HINT: The purple arm never angles to the left.

FIND where each detail appears in the big picture.

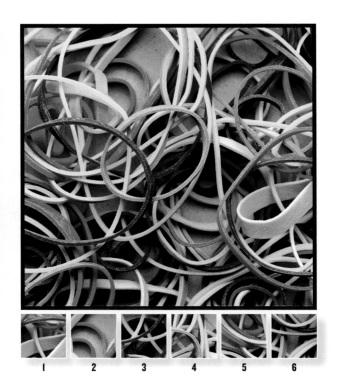

1   2   3   4   5   6

HINT: Detail 1 is along the right edge.

PUT the numbers in the boxes so every row, column, and main diagonal adds up to the same number.

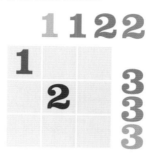

HINT: The sum is 6.

HERE are two different ways to fit four pieces into a black box. What is the total number of ways to fit these four pieces into the box?

HINT: First place the big black square, then place other pieces around it.

PUZZLE TYPE: WORD
COMPLETION: ☐

DIFFICULTY: ✹✹
TIME: ________

IN THIS CROSSWORD each letter reads in two directions. Copy letters from the alphabet at top into the empty boxes. You may rotate and flip letters. Each word reads in the direction of its clue. The first letter is given.

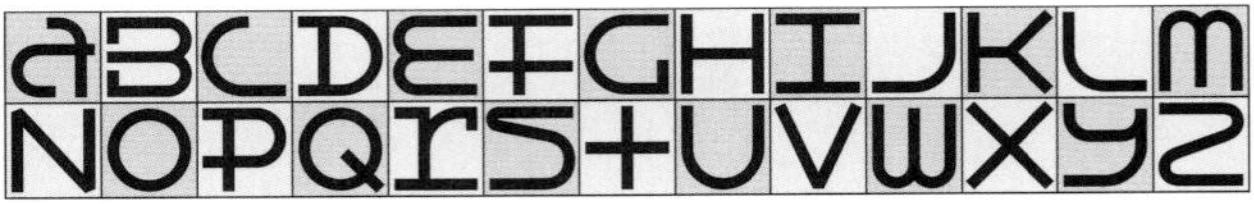
A B C D E F G H I J K L M
N O P Q R S T U V W X Y Z

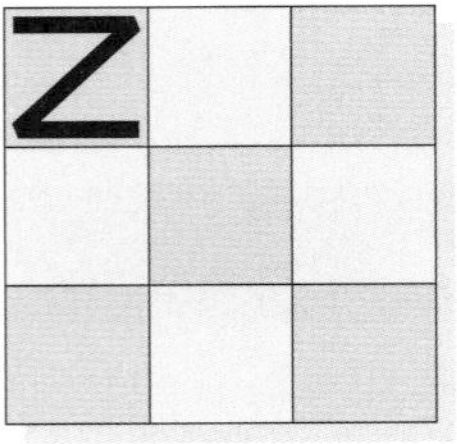
Z
pimple
arrow launcher
wholesome grain
possess
Homer Simpson noise
brewed drink

HINT: The answer to "pimple" is "zit."

LAY SIX SHEETS of stationery flat on a table so each sheet overlaps above exactly one other sheet, and overlaps below exactly one other sheet. Sheets may not be folded, cut, or bent.

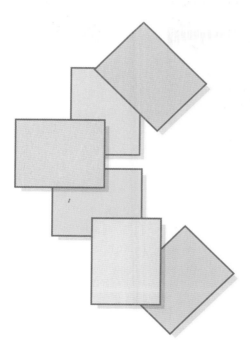

HINT: There are two different solutions.

FIND where each detail appears in the big picture.

| 1 | 2 | 3 | 4 | 5 | 6 |

HINT: Detail 1 is right of middle.

HOW do the figures on the left differ from the figures on the right?

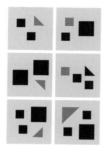 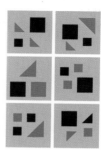

HINT: See the world through rose-colored glasses.

HERE are two different ways to fit four pieces into a black box. What is the total number of ways to fit these four pieces into the box?

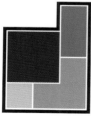 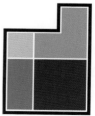

HINT: First place the big black square, then place other pieces around it.

| PUZZLE TYPE: WORD | DIFFICULTY: ✿✿ |
| COMPLETION: ▢ | TIME: _____ |

FIND 17 words of four or more letters, spelled forward or backward, straight or diagonal, that combine with LINE to make a common word or phrase. The leftover letters spell a relevant quotation.

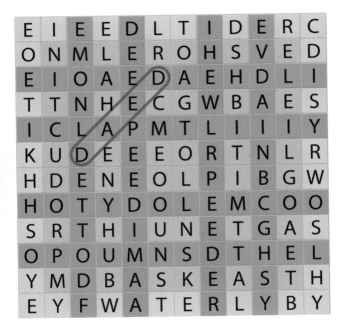

E	I	E	E	D	L	T	I	D	E	R	C
O	N	M	L	E	R	O	H	S	V	E	D
E	I	O	A	E	D	A	E	H	D	L	I
T	T	N	H	E	C	G	W	B	A	E	S
I	C	L	A	P	M	T	L	I	I	I	Y
K	U	D	E	E	E	O	R	T	N	L	R
H	D	E	N	E	O	L	P	I	B	G	W
H	O	T	Y	D	O	L	E	M	C	O	O
S	R	T	H	I	U	N	E	T	G	A	S
O	P	O	U	M	N	S	D	T	H	E	L
Y	M	D	B	A	S	K	E	A	S	T	H
E	Y	F	W	A	T	E	R	L	Y	B	Y

HINT: The longest hidden word is "electrical."

MATCH EACH DETAIL with a different letter. For instance, detail 6 is from the R. All details are right side up and magnified the same amount.

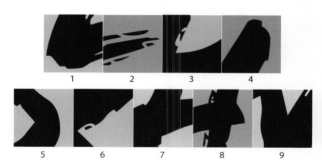

RAINCLOUD

6 ___ ___ ___ ___ ___ ___ ___ ___

1   2   3   4

5   6   7   8   9

PUZZLE TYPE: VISUAL	DIFFICULTY: ✸
COMPLETION: ☐	TIME: _____

FIND where each detail appears in the big picture.

| 1 | 2 | 3 | 4 | 5 | 6 |

HINT: Detail 1 is in the left middle.

138. BY ANALOGY

EACH EQUATION below uses the same rule to combine letters of two words to make a third word. Figure out the rule, then fill in the missing word.

> **SEAT** + **AGAR** = **STAR**
>
> **POOL** + **PROD** = **PLOD**
>
> **ACHE** + **HEAD** = **CHAD**
>
> **PORE** + **STAY** =

HINT: Ignore vowels.

139. ASSEMBLIES

HERE are two different ways to fit four pieces into a black box. What is the total number of ways to fit these four pieces into the box?

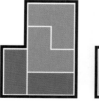
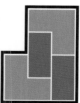

HINT: First place the two L-shaped pieces, then fit the green pieces around them.

FILL IN the missing words to turn LEAF into TREE. Each word differs from the previous word in just one letter, like this: THIS–THIN–THAN–THAT.

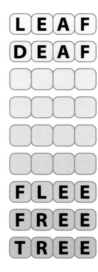

LEAF
DEAF
☐☐☐☐
☐☐☐☐
☐☐☐☐
☐☐☐☐
FLEE
FREE
TREE

HINT: Change the last letter of DEAF to D.

HOW can four people join their hands to make a knotted loop that looks like this?

Photo by Steve Dibartolomeo

HINT: Each person stands at one corner of this rectangular knot. All arms stay straight.

DRIVING to work one day you notice that the mileage indicators show the interesting pair of numbers 12345.6 and 123.4. The odometer at top shows the mileage since the car was manufactured, while the trip meter at bottom shows the mileage since it was last reset to 000.0.

Coincidentally, the digits on the trip meter are the first four digits of the odometer. How far must you drive before this happens again? You are not allowed to reset the trip meter. (If you are allowed to reset the trip meter, there is a better answer.)

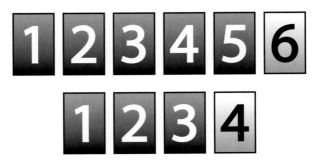

Puzzle by Harry Nelson

HINT: The first two digits of both numbers will be 13.

DRIVING to work one day you notice that the mileage indicators show the interesting pair of numbers 12345.6 and 123.4.

What is the shortest distance you can drive before the ten places in the two meters show all ten digits 0 to 9? Easier question: How far must you drive if you can reset the trip meter to 0 at any time? And if driving backward reverses the odometers, can you improve your answers to the previous questions?

HINT: You must drive forward between 700 and 1,000 miles. If you are allowed to reset the trip meter, you can drive forward less than 100 miles.

SUPPOSE you got in a car that started with an odometer reading of 000,000,000.0 and drove 2 billion miles, during which time the odometer returned to all 0s twice. (Presumably you are driving very fast or have a very long lifetime.) What is the longest distance during which the odometer would never show all 10 digits?

HINT: While you are driving the longest such distance, the odometer will pass through 000,000,000.0 again.

WHAT COMMON THEME connects all three of these images? The answer may involve wordplay.

HINT: arc

FILL EACH GRID so every row, column, and colored region contains one of each number 1 to 6.

4					
	5				
3				1	
5		3	★		
		2			
				6	2

		5			
		★		6	
5		2	3		
	2	4			
4		3	1		

Puzzles by Michael Rios

HINT: In the top puzzle, the star must be a 4 because every other number appears in the same row, column, or region. In the bottom puzzle, the star must be a 1 because every other number appears in the same row or column.

PUT the seven digits in the empty boxes to make a correct sum.

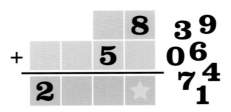

HINT: The 4 goes in the box with the star.

UNSCRAMBLE the letters in each word pair to make two new words with opposite meanings, like "on vs. off."

| **RARE FAN** = _____ vs. _____ |
| **EVER ROUND** = _____ vs. _____ |
| **GALLON HINT** = _____ vs. _____ |
| **SECOND POLE** = _____ vs. _____ |

HINT: distance, weaving, winner take, store sign

HOW MANY times does the shape at right appear in the figure below, at any size or angle?

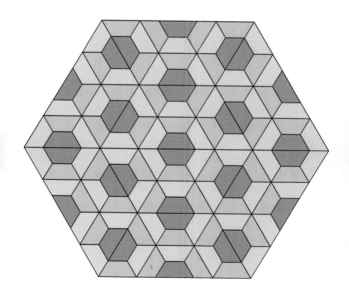

HINT: Figures at each size are made of four of the next smaller size. No figure crosses over the "equator."

WHAT COMMON THEME
connects all three
of these images?
The answer may
involve wordplay.

HINT: inventions

HOW DO the letters on the left differ from the letters on the right?

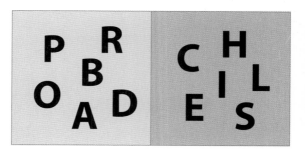

HINT: Pay attention to the shapes of the letters.

PUT the seven digits in the empty boxes to make a correct sum.

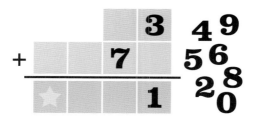

HINT: The 6 goes in the box with the star.

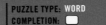

PUZZLE TYPE: WORD
COMPLETION: ⬜

DIFFICULTY: ✿ ✿
TIME: _____

DECODE these two familiar phrases.

MOONCEON

WITHNV

154. COVER STORY

PUZZLE TYPE: SPATIAL
COMPLETION: ☐
DIFFICULTY: ✹✹
TIME: ______

UNSCRAMBLE each set of nine tiles to spell the name of a famous written work. The two works are related. Do not rotate tiles.

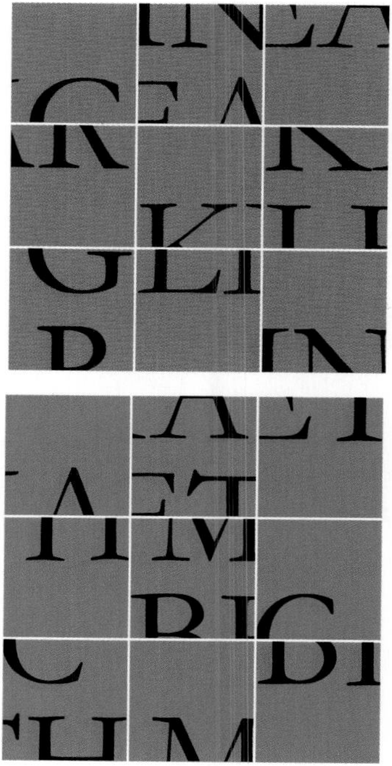

HINT: Both works were written by William Shakespeare.

WHAT COMMON THEME connects all four of these images?

HINT: The duck picture represents "water."

ABE AND BARB sat in the same row. Carl sat straight behind Deb. Ed sat farther forward than Barb and farther right than Carl. Where did Fay sit?

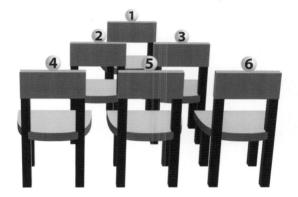

HINT: If Carl sat straight behind Deb, then where did Carl sit?

157. CAN YOU DIGIT

PUT the six digits in the empty boxes to make a correct sum.

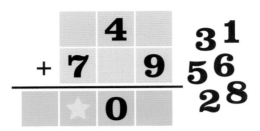

158. SECRET WORD

DEDUCE the secret five-letter word from the clues. For instance, the word WRITE shares three letter tiles with the word RIGHT.

The secret word

☐ ☐ ☐ ☐ ☐

shares no tiles with

E P O C H

and shares four tiles with

T U M O R

WHICH TWO patterns look the same when folded into cubes?

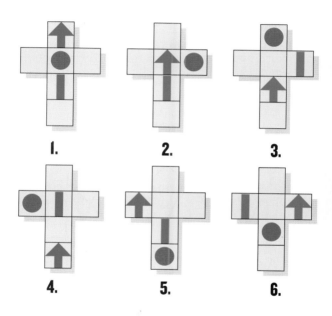

1.

2.

3.

4.

5.

6.

THE DIAGRAM below shows which of the eight major blood types can donate blood to which other types. For instance, one arrow shows that a person with blood type A− can donate blood to a person with type A+. Note that compatibility does not work both ways: A− can donate to A+, but not vice versa.

    1. Which type can donate to the most other blood types? Which type can receive the most other types of blood?

    2. Make a chain of four blood types so the first can donate to the second, the second to the third, and the third to the fourth. How many solutions can you find?

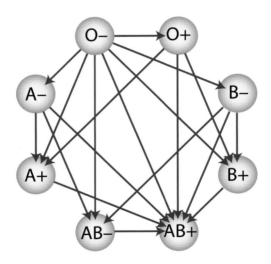

HINT: The blood type that can donate to the most other blood types has the most arrows leaving it. Every chain of four blood types begins with O− and ends with AB+.

THE SIX unassuming words at right have an extraordinary property: every pair of words shares exactly one letter. For instance, ADO and ORE share the letter O, and ORE and BAR share the letter R. There is a seventh word that completes the set. Can you discover it by studying the triangular diagram?

ADO
ORE
BAR
BOY
YEA
BED

— — —

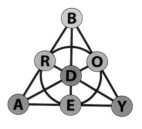

HINT: Every word is composed of letters that lie on a single line (straight or circular) in the diagram.

HERE ARE other sets of words in which every pair of words shares the same number of letters. For instance, each pair of words in set 2 shares two letters. Can you fill in the missing words?

1.	2.	3.
TOE	NAIL	RATES
USE	SALE	CASTE
STY	SINE	CARTS
YOU	IDEA	CARES
YEN	SLID	CRATE
	SAND	
— — —	— — — —	— — — — —

HINT: Pairs of words in set 1 share one letter; pairs of words in set 3 share four letters.

WHICH TWO figures match perfectly? Figures may be rotated.

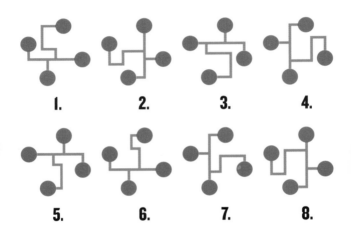

1.   **2.**   **3.**   **4.**

5.   **6.**   **7.**   **8.**

HINT: The two matching figures do not include figure 5 or figure 6.

164. GRID LOGIC

PUT the numbers in the boxes so that multiplying the three numbers in each row, column, and main diagonal always yields the same number.

12

3 4

6
9
12
18
36

HINT: The product of each row is $2 \times 2 \times 2 \times 3 \times 3 \times 3$.

165. CAN YOU DIGIT

PUT the six digits in the empty boxes to make a correct equation.

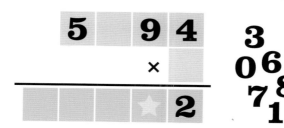

5 | | **9 4**

× | |

───────────

| ★ | **2**

3
0 6
7 8
1

HINT: The 8 goes in the box with the star.

THESE WELL-KNOWN SAYINGS were translated by a computer to another language, then back into English, with surprising results. What were the original sayings?

> Practical what you declare.
>
> From the view, from the brain.
>
> The money is the carrot of already angry.
>
> Water functions always deeply.
>
> It never does not say the dice.

HINT: What is a five-letter word for "always" that starts with S?

PUZZLE TYPE: SPATIAL	DIFFICULTY: ✹✹
COMPLETION: ☐	TIME: _____

FIND a path from the top arrow to the bottom arrow that follows the repeating pattern: ●●●●. You may move left, right, up, or down from one dot to the next. The orange path, for instance, ends at a dead end.

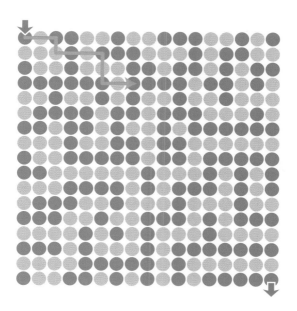

HINT: Start right, right, down, right, right, right, up.

WHICH TWO figures match perfectly? Figures may *not* be rotated.

1.

2.   **3.**

4.

5.

6.   **7.**

8.

HINT: The two matching figures do not include figure 1 or figure 2.

HOW do the figures on the left differ from the figures on the right?

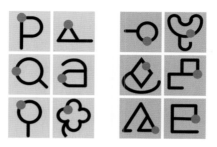

HINT: Where's the dot?

PUT the seven digits in the empty boxes to make a correct sum.

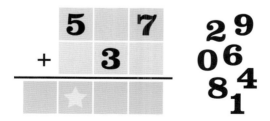

HINT: The 0 goes in the box with the star.

FIND 29 words spelled forward or backward, straight or diagonal, that combine with BALL to make a word or phrase. The leftover letters spell a relevant quotation.

T	N	A	M	E	K	M	E	P	A	N	E
E	S	A	E	R	G	I	M	A	P	E	R
O	L	A	R	A	O	Y	C	R	W	H	O
W	I	K	F	C	O	W	E	K	P	A	G
S	M	S	C	Q	F	I	E	L	D	E	A
V	E	E	P	U	R	E	A	R	L	R	M
S	M	T	A	E	N	Y	R	I	C	O	E
U	C	O	H	T	E	K	S	A	B	S	V
K	G	T	O	R	G	D	N	H	A	S	R
B	E	O	I	R	D	N	A	B	T	N	U
T	F	F	W	Y	O	R	A	C	A	O	C
N	N	O	N	N	D	B	A	L	L	W	M

WHICH SHAPES below can be made by cutting the shape at right into two pieces and reassembling?

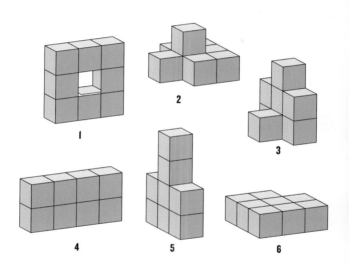

I

2

3

4

5

6

HINT: Of the six shapes given, there is just one that cannot be assembled.

WHICH TWO figures match perfectly? Figures may be rotated.

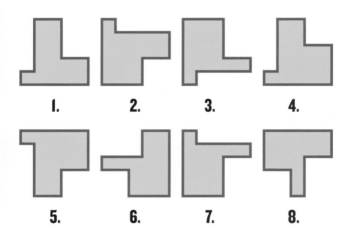

1.　　　　2.　　　　3.　　　　4.

5.　　　　6.　　　　7.　　　　8.

HINT: The two matching figures do not include figure 7 or figure 8.

174. BY ANALOGY

FIGURE OUT at least two good answers for each alphabetic analogy.

1. ABC is to ABD as
   XYZ is to **XYA**

2. EQE is to QEQ as
   RVVVR is to _____

3. FG is to GH as
   FFG is to _____

4. GFF is to GGF as
   AAABB is to _____

HINT: A is the first letter of the alphabet and Z is the last.

175. CAN YOU DIGIT

PUT the eight digits in the empty boxes to make a correct equation.

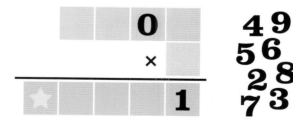

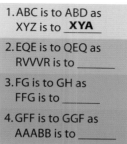

HINT: The 6 goes in the box with the star.

FILL IN the missing words to turn FROWN into SMILE. Each word differs from the previous word in just one letter, like this: THIS–THIN–THAN–THAT. There is more than one solution.

HINT: Change the fourth letter of SLOWS.

LAY SIX SHEETS of stationery in two layers, flat on a table, so each sheet touches every other sheet. Sheets may not be folded, cut, or bent. At most, three sheets may touch at one corner.

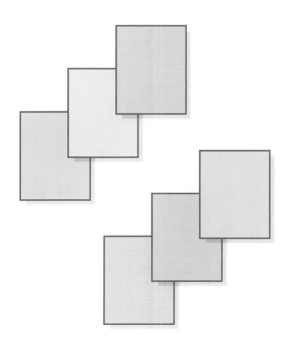

GEOBOARDS are square boards used to teach geometry. By snapping rubber bands around the 25 pegs, students can make shapes. Which of the following shapes can you make on a geoboard? For instance, the illustration shows a triangle with five interior pegs.

1. Triangle with five interior pegs.
2. Triangle with six interior pegs.
3. Triangle with seven interior pegs.
4. Square with area 4.
5. Square with area 5.
6. Square with area 6.

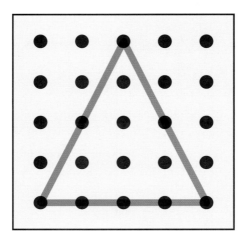

HINT: Two of the constructions are not possible. Squares can be tilted at an angle.

WHICH of the following shapes can you make on a geoboard? For instance, the illustration shows how to make shape 5.

1. Pentagon with all sides same length.
2. Hexagon with no sides parallel.
3. Hexagon with three sides parallel to one another.
4. Hexagon with four sides parallel to one another.
5. Hexagon with all sides different lengths.
6. Hexagon with all sides the same length.

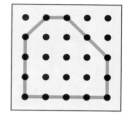

HINT: Two of the constructions are not possible.

WHICH of the following shapes can you make on a geoboard? For instance, the illustration shows how to make shape 3. A concave shape has at least one inward-pointing angle. A convex shape has no such angle.

1. A heptagon with all seven sides congruent.
2. An octagon with all eight sides congruent.
3. A concave nonagon (nine sides).
4. A convex nonagon (nine sides).
5. A concave 24-gon.
6. A concave 25-gon.

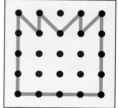

HINT: Two of the constructions are not possible.

FIND where each detail appears in the big picture.

| 1 | 2 | 3 | 4 | 5 | 6 |

HINT: Detail 1 is in the middle right.

FILL EACH GRID so every row, column, and colored region contains one of each number 1 to 6. Each marked diagonal must also contain one of each number 1 to 6.

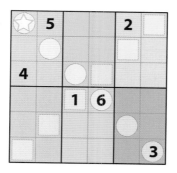

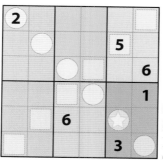

Puzzles by Michael Rios

HINT: In the top puzzle, the star must be a 1 because every other number appears in the same row, column, or diagonal. In the bottom puzzle, the star must be a 4 because every other number appears in the same row, column, region, or diagonal.

PUT the eight digits in the empty boxes to make a correct equation.

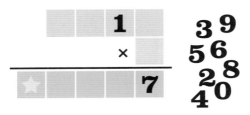

THESE TITLES of classic movies were translated by a computer to another language, then back into English, with surprising results. What were the original titles?

NOISE OF MUSIC (1965)

MINE JUST MRS. (1964)

OCCIDENTAL LATERAL HISTORY (1961)

IT CLOSES THE MEETING OF THE THIRD AMIABLE (1977)

MATCH EACH DETAIL with a different letter. For instance, detail 4 is from the G. All details are right side up and magnified the same amount.

HINT: Detail 8 is from the E.

FIND where each detail appears in the big picture.

1 2 3 4 5 6

HINT: Detail 1 is in the upper left.

187. SEEK WHENCE

PUZZLE TYPE: LOGIC
COMPLETION: ☐
DIFFICULTY: ✱✱✱
TIME: ________

EXPLAIN why the sequence

2 1 2 2 2 3...

could be logically continued as any of the following:

A ...2 4 2 5 2 6

B ...2 3 4 2 4 5

C ... 4 4 2 5 6 6

For instance, the sequence **1 2 1 2 3**
could be continued as the expanding sequence
(1 2) (1 2 3) (1 2 3 4) (1 2 3 4 5) . . .
or as the paired sequence
(1 2) (1 2) (3 4) (3 4) (5 6) (5 6) . . .

HINT: Group the third sequence as (2 1 2 2) (2 3 4 4) (2 5 6 6) . . .

PUT the six digits in the empty boxes to make a correct equation.

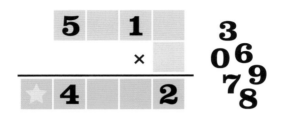

HINT: The 3 goes in the box with the star.

DECODE these two familiar phrases.

| STORM
TH | C
STORY |

HINT: above and below

THESE TWO people are holding hands. What happens if the man in red uncrosses his arms without letting go of the other man's hands?

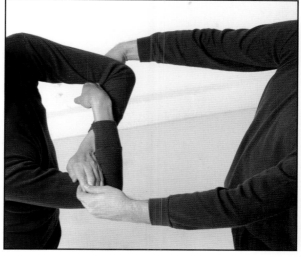

Photo by Steve Dibartolomeo

HINT: Cross your arms and pick up the ends of a piece of string.

FIND where each detail appears in the big picture.

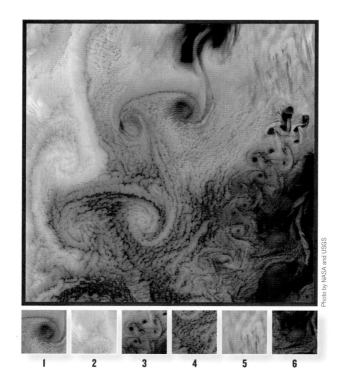

Photo by NASA and USGS

1   2   3   4   5   6

HINT: Detail 1 is just above the middle.

EACH LETTER in the sum stands for a different digit. For instance, the letter O equals 5. Can you find the values of the other letters? If a letter appears more than once, it always stands for the same digit. The first digit of a number is never 0. Use logic to deduce digits: Why must A equal 8?

HINT: Note that there must have been a carryover from the thousands to ten thousands place, since the A in AGONY is not the same digit as the G in GUILT. Similarly, there must have been a carryover from the hundreds to the thousands place in order to turn the G in AGONY into the U in GUILT. Therefore, the G in AGONY must be a 9, since any lesser value would not cause a carryover to the ten thousands place. And so the A in AGONY must be an 8, in order to add up to the G = 9 in GUILT.

PUT the seven digits in the empty boxes to make a correct equation.

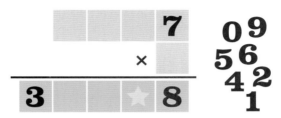

DEDUCE the secret five-letter word from the clues. For instance, the word WRITE shares three letter tiles with the word RIGHT.

The secret word

☐ ☐ ☐ ☐ ☐

shares three tiles with

B O U G H

and shares three tiles with

C H A R D

HOW MANY cubes of any size can you find in the figure? For instance, the whole figure is a 3 × 3 × 3 cube, and the smallest cube is 1 × 1 × 1. To get you started, one cube has been highlighted.

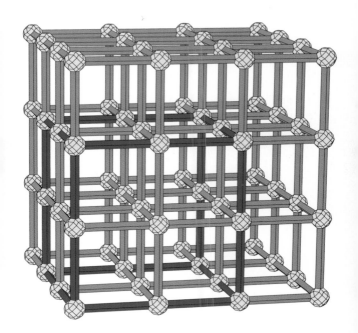

HINT: Cubes come in three sizes: 1 × 1 × 1, 2 × 2 × 2, and 3 × 3 × 3.

MANY BRANCHES of science have names that end with *ology*, meaning "the study of." For instance, *biology* is the study of living things, from the Greek *bios*, meaning "life." Can you match each of the "ologies" below with the subject that it studies?

I. Agrology	a. Bells
2. Campanology	b. Causes or origins
3. Cetology	c. Cells
4. Cytology	d. Sign language
5. Dactylology	e. Soil for crops
6. Dendrology	f. Trees
7. Etiology	g. Whales

HINT: The word *campanology* is related to *campanile*. The word *cytology* is related to *cytoplasm*. The word *etiology* is related to *etymology*.

CAN YOU match each of the "ologies" below with the subject that it studies?

1. Geomorphology	5. Mycology	a. Eggs	e. Mushrooms
2. Lithology	6. Myology	b. Land forms	f. Rocks
3. Meteorology	7. Oology	c. Measurement	g. Weather
4. Metrology		d. Muscles	

HINT: The word *lithology* is related to *monolith*. The word *oology* is related to *ovum*.

CAN YOU match each of the "ologies" below with the subject that it studies?

1. Pomology	5. Speleology	a. Caves	e. Nose
2. Rhinology	6. Vexillology	b. Flags	f. Signs
3. Selenology	7. Vulcanology	c. Fruit	g. Volcanoes
4. Semiology		d. Moon	

HINT: The word *pomology* is related to *pomegranate*. The word *rhinology* is related to *rhinoceros* and *rhinoplasty*. The word *vulcanology* is related to *Vulcan*, the Roman god of fire.

| PUZZLE TYPE: VISUAL | DIFFICULTY: ✿ ✿ |
| COMPLETION: ☐ | TIME: _____ |

WHAT COMMON THEME connects all three of these images? The answer may involve wordplay.

HINT: first five letters.

PUT the letters in the boxes so every row and column spells a common word.

HINT: The letter Y goes in the lower right corner.

PUT the five digits in the empty boxes to make a correct equation.

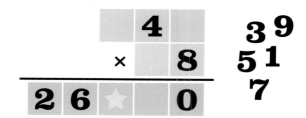

HINT: The 9 goes in the box with the star.

IN THIS CROSSWORD each letter reads in two directions. Copy letters from the alphabet at top into the empty boxes. You may rotate and flip letters. Each word reads in the direction of its clue. The first letter is given.

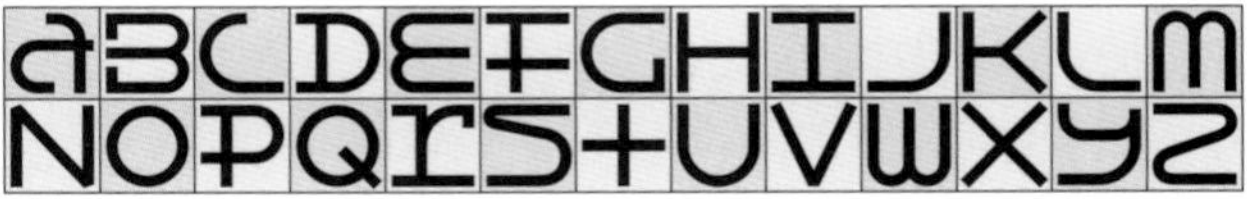

ABCDEFGHIJKLM
NOPQRSTUVWXYZ

shall

heavy weight

fast plane

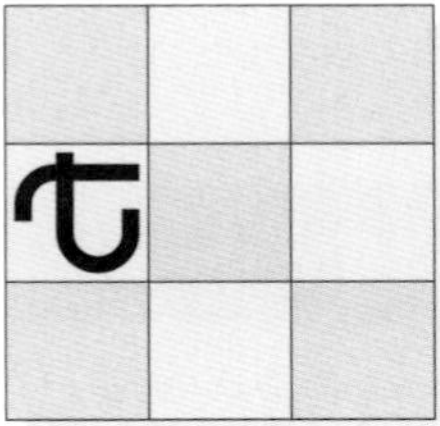

research center

hip, cool

inquire

UNSCRAMBLE each set of nine tiles to spell the name of a famous written work. The two works are related. Do not rotate tiles.

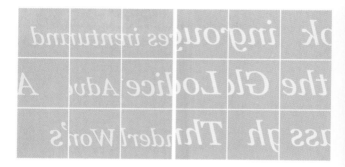

| PUZZLE TYPE: VISUAL | DIFFICULTY: ☼ |
| COMPLETION: ☐ | TIME: _____ |

WHAT COMMON THEME connects all three of these images? The answer may involve wordplay.

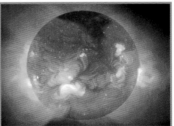

HINT: pointed shape

HOW do the figures on the left differ from the figures on the right?

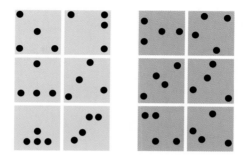

HINT: Line them up.

PUT the seven digits in the empty boxes to make a correct sum.

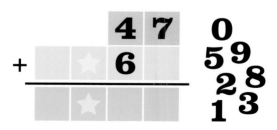

HINT: The stars must be a 9 and a 0.

FIND 29 words spelled forward or backward, straight or diagonal, that combine with HOUSE to make a common word or phrase. The leftover letters spell a relevant quotation.

HINT: The longest word is "slaughter."

WHICH TWO patterns look the same when folded into cubes?

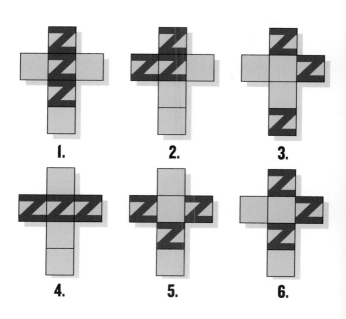

1.   **2.**   **3.**

4.   **5.**   **6.**

HINT: Pattern 1 is not one of the two matching patterns.

WHAT COMMON THEME
connects all three
of these images?
The answer may
involve wordplay.

HINT: It's a cinch.

EACH EQUATION below uses the same rule to combine letters of two words to make a third word. Figure out the rule, then fill in the missing word.

SEAT + AGAR = STAR

HOPE + AIR = HEAR

FOR + LAST = FLAT

BY + RIDE =

HINT: First run the two words together.

PUT the seven digits in the empty boxes to make a correct equation.

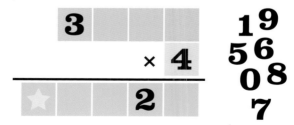

HINT: The star must be a 1.

FILL IN the missing words to turn BEACH into WAVES. Each word differs from the previous word in just one letter, like this: THIS–THIN–THAN–THAT.

B E A C H

⬜ ⬜ ⬜ ⬜ ⬜

⬜ ⬜ ⬜ ⬜ ⬜

⬜ ⬜ ⬜ ⬜ ⬜

⬜ ⬜ ⬜ ⬜ ⬜

M A R C S

M A R E S

W A R E S

W A V E S

HINT: Change the first letter of BEACH to P.

FIND a path from the top arrow to the bottom arrow that follows the repeating pattern: ●●●●●●●. You may move left, right, up, or down from one dot to the next. Do not visit a dot more than once. The orange path, for instance, ends at a dead end.

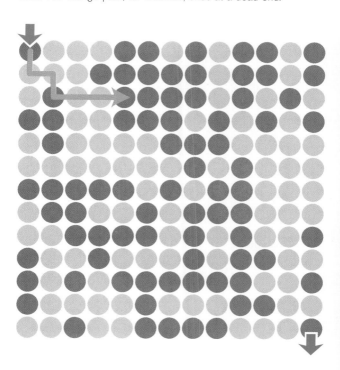

HINT: Start by going down as far as possible.

| PUZZLE TYPE: SPATIAL | DIFFICULTY: ☀ |
| COMPLETION: ▢ | TIME: _____ |

PATTERN BLOCKS are colorful wooden blocks used by teachers to teach symmetry and fractions. Here is a shape made of 13 pattern blocks. Can you find another way to make the same shape using exactly the same blocks, but with every block in a different position?

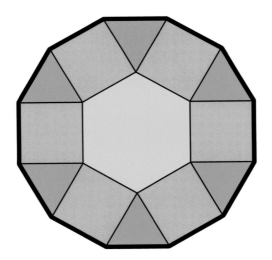

HINT: Turn the hexagon.

Here is a shape made of five pattern blocks. Can you find another way to make the same shape using exactly the same blocks, but with every block in a different position?

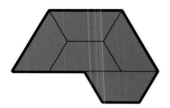

HINT: How else can you fit a block in the lower left corner?

At right is a shape made of six pattern blocks. Can you find another way to make the same shape using exactly the same blocks, but with every block in a different position?

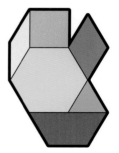

HINT: Move the yellow hexagon to the bottom.

WHICH TWO figures match perfectly?

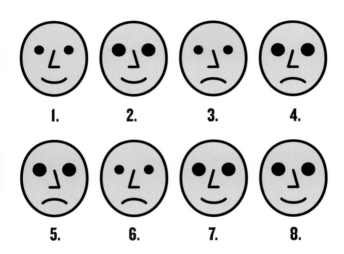

1. 2. 3. 4.

5. 6. 7. 8.

HINT: The two matching figures do not include figure 5 or figure 6.

FILL EACH GRID so every row, column, and colored region contains one of each number 1 to 6.

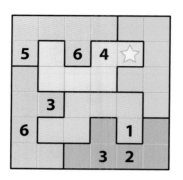

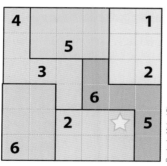

Puzzles by Michael Rios

HINT: In the top puzzle, the star must be a 3 because every other number appears in the same row or column. In the bottom puzzle, the star must be a 6 because this is the only place you can place a 6 in the orange region.

PUT the seven digits in the empty boxes to make a correct equation.

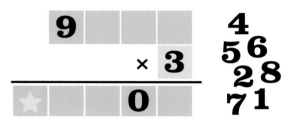

UNSCRAMBLE the letters in each word pair to make two new related words. All pairs follow the same theme.

BUSY ELK = _____ + _____

TAMED ROOT = _____ + _____

EGG SNARERS = _____ + _____

CORN ALLEYWAY = _____ + _____

WHICH SHAPES below can be made by rotating and overlapping the two pieces at right? You may not flip pieces over.

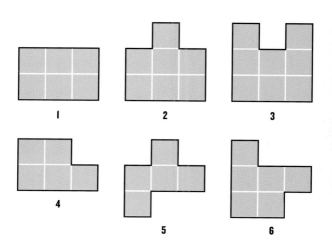

1

2

3

4

5

6

HINT: Of the six shapes, two cannot be made.

WHICH TWO figures match perfectly? Some figures may be rotated.

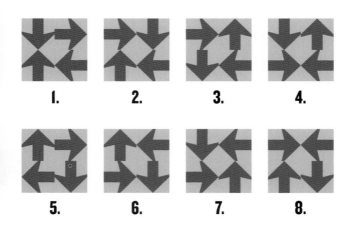

1.   **2.**   **3.**   **4.**

5.   **6.**   **7.**   **8.**

HINT: The two matching figures do not include figure 3 or figure 4.

223. CATEGORIES

| PUZZLE TYPE: LOGIC | DIFFICULTY: ✿ ✿ |
| COMPLETION: ☐ | TIME: _____ |

HOW do the letters on the left differ from the letters on the right?

HINT: Imagine folding each letter in half.

224. CAN YOU DIGIT

| PUZZLE TYPE: NUMBER | DIFFICULTY: ✿ ✿ |
| COMPLETION: ☐ | TIME: _____ |

PUT the seven digits in the empty boxes to make a correct sum. There is more than one solution.

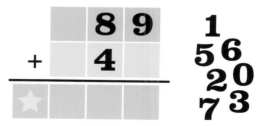

HINT: The star must be a 1.

DECODE these two familiar phrases.

LAY SIX sheets of stationery flat on a table so each sheet overlaps above exactly two other sheets, and overlaps below exactly two other sheets. Sheets may not be folded, cut, or bent.

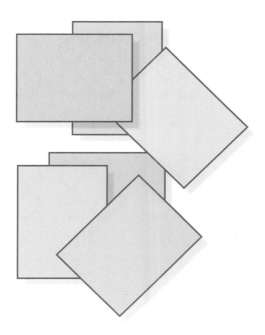

HINT: The solution has hexagonal symmetry.

WHICH TWO figures match perfectly? Figures may not be rotated.

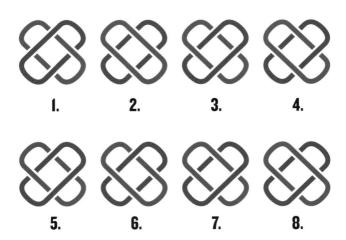

1. **2.** **3.** **4.**

5. **6.** **7.** **8.**

HINT: The two matching figures do not include figure 1 or figure 2.

ABE, BARB, AND CARL sat with no two of them next to each other. Deb sat directly opposite Abe. Barb sat in the red seat. Ed sat just to Barb's right. Where did Fay sit?

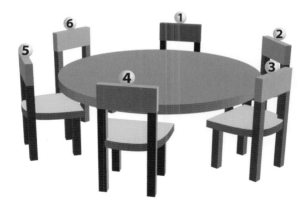

HINT: Abe, Barb, and Carl must have sat at the corners of a big triangle.

PUT the six digits in the empty boxes to make a correct equation.

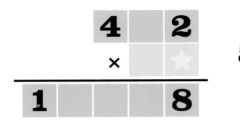

DEDUCE the secret five-letter word from the clues. For instance, WRITE shares three letter tiles with RIGHT.

The secret word

shares three tiles with

A D U L T

and shares four tiles with

G U L C H

MATCH EACH DETAIL with a different letter. For instance, detail 7 is from the F. All details are right side up and magnified the same amount.

FELDSPAR

7 ___ ___ ___ ___ ___ ___ ___

1 2 3 4

5 6 7 8

THE TINY NATION of Yewessay has a population of 121, divided into 11 states of 11 citizens each. Each year the citizens vote on two candidates for president. First, each citizen votes for one candidate. Then the candidate who gets more votes in a state receives one electoral college vote for that state. The candidate who receives more electoral college votes becomes president.

As in U.S. presidential elections, strange things can happen. What is the largest number of popular votes a candidate can receive and not become president?

HINT: To lose the election, the candidate must lose at least six states.

233. VOTE-OLOGY B

What is the largest number of states a candidate can win and not win the popular vote?

HINT: The smallest margin by which a candidate can win a state is six votes to five.

234. VOTE-OLOGY C

SUPPOSE you can divide the 121 citizens of Yewessay into any number of states. Each state must contain at least one person. If each state contributes one electoral college vote, what is the largest number of popular votes a candidate can receive and not become president?

HINT: In the most extreme case, there are just three states.

| PUZZLE TYPE: VISUAL | DIFFICULTY: ✿ ✿ ✿ |
| COMPLETION: ☐ | TIME: _____ |

FIND where each detail appears in the big picture.

Photo by John and Karen Hollingsworth

1   2   3   4   5   6

HINT: Detail 1 is near the right edge.

236. BOOKSHELF

REARRANGE the order of the books so adjacent book titles are either the same length or share a common letter, and the leftmost book is red.

HINT: Book 4 (PUSHUP) must be next to book 1 (DIESEL).

237. DOT MATRIX

HOW MANY dots will be in the next figure in the sequence below?

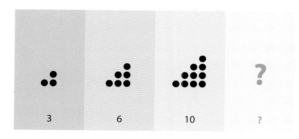

| 3 | 6 | 10 | ? |

HINT: Each successive figure adds a new column of dots on the right.

THESE WELL-KNOWN SAYINGS were translated by a computer to another language, then back into English, with surprising results. What were the original sayings?

> It hits while the iron is warm.
>
> Initially come, initially been useful.
>
> As for evidence of the pudding there are times when you eat.
>
> More than one road it removed the skin from the tomcat.
>
> Is human to mad.

HINT: What is a three-letter word for "road"?

HOW can these three people hold hands to make a knotted loop that looks like this?

Photo by Steve Dibartolomeo

HINT: Everyone does the same thing. Cross your right arm over your neighbor's left.

| PUZZLE TYPE: VISUAL | DIFFICULTY: ☀ |
| COMPLETION: ☐ | TIME: _____ |

FIND where each detail appears in the big picture.

1   2   3   4   5   6

HINT: Detail 1 is in the lower middle.

HOW do the figures on the left differ from the figures on the right?

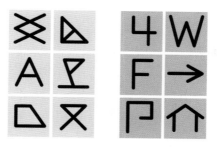

HINT: It's what's inside that counts.

HOW MANY dots will be in the next figure in the sequence below?

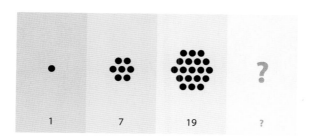

1   7   19   ?

HINT: Each successive figure adds a new ring of dots around the outside.

FIND 30 words spelled forward or backward, straight or diagonal, that combine with FOOT to make a common word or phrase. The leftover letters spell a relevant quotation.

W	O	R	K	S	D	L	O	H	T	E	R
A	K	E	A	T	O	N	L	I	Y	S	A
P	I	C	T	E	A	U	R	L	E	O	C
L	E	A	D	P	W	L	O	L	S	O	E
S	T	E	A	A	L	O	F	A	U	L	T
O	N	L	L	Y	T	T	R	F	O	I	O
M	L	L	Y	S	S	U	P	C	E	T	N
L	E	L	B	R	R	T	K	R	E	A	V
E	S	O	A	A	N	E	H	N	E	L	Y
F	E	E	T	B	R	I	D	G	E	S	O
O	G	T	H	P	R	E	I	N	I	N	T
T	A	T	N	I	R	P	S	B	U	L	C

HINT: The longest word is "bridges."

HOW MANY triangles of any size appear in the three-dimensional figure? To get you started, one triangle has been highlighted.

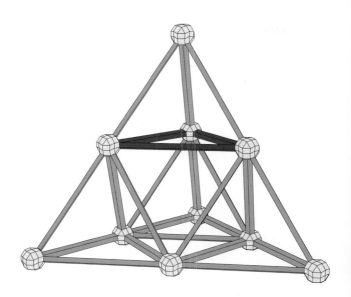

HINT: Triangles appear in two sizes.

PUZZLE TYPE: VISUAL	DIFFICULTY: ✹ ✹
COMPLETION: ☐	TIME: _____

FIND where each detail appears in the big picture.

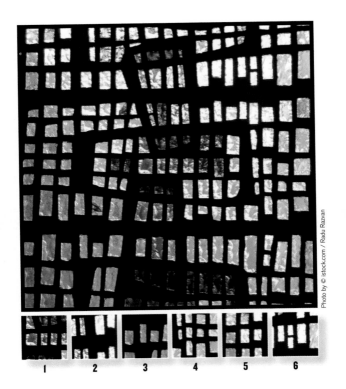

Photo by © istock.com / Radu Razvan

1   2   3   4   5   6

HINT: Detail 1 is in the middle.

246. BY ANALOGY

PUZZLE TYPE: LOGIC
COMPLETION: ☐

DIFFICULTY: ✿✿
TIME: _____

EACH EQUATION below uses the same rule to combine letters of two words to make a third word. Figure out the rule, then fill in the missing word.

$$THIS + NOSE = TINS$$

$$ALSO + ERA = ASEA$$

$$TAR + HERE = TREE$$

$$SLANG + GAIN =$$

HINT: First run the two words together.

247. DOT MATRIX

PUZZLE TYPE: NUMBER
COMPLETION: ☐

DIFFICULTY: ✿✿
TIME: _____

HOW MANY dots will be in the next figure in the sequence below?

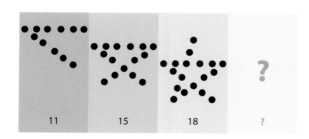

| 11 | 15 | 18 | ? |

HINT: What dots must you add to complete the star?

WRITE A LETTER in each bubble to spell words that fit the clues. The first word is given. Then rearrange all the letters in the gold bubbles to make a word that ends with OVE.

ove **N** hot place for cooking
ove ⚪⚪ apparent, obvious
ove ⚪⚪⚪ put in more effort than necessary
ove ⚪⚪⚪⚪ excess, surplus
ove ⚪⚪⚪⚪⚪ musical introduction
ove ⚪⚪⚪⚪⚪⚪ high gear
ove ⚪⚪⚪⚪⚪⚪⚪ completely defeats
ove ⚪⚪⚪⚪⚪⚪⚪⚪ think too hard about

⚪⚪⚪⚪⚪⚪⚪⚪ tree

HINT: From top to bottom, the gold bubbles contain the letters N, R, O, G, E, V, M, A.

UNSCRAMBLE each set of nine tiles to spell the name of a famous written work. The two works are related. Do not rotate tiles.

HINT: Both works were written by James Joyce.

PUZZLE TYPE: SPATIAL   DIFFICULTY: ✸✸
COMPLETION: ☐   TIME: _____

DRAW an equilateral triangle, using only a straightedge (unmarked ruler) for drawing straight lines and a compass for drawing circles of any size. Here is a method from Euclid's classic geometry text *The Elements*.

1. Given two points A and B, use the straightedge to draw line segment AB.

A   B

2. Use the compass to draw a circle with center A and radius AB.

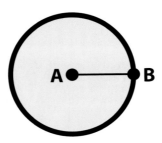

A●━━━━●B

Can you complete the last three steps of the construction?

HINT: The next step is to draw another circle.

251. EUCLID B

DRAW a square using only a straightedge and compass. Here is a method from *The Elements*.
1. Given two points A and B, use the straightedge to draw segment AB.
2–3. Use the compass to draw a circle with center A and radius AB, and another circle with center B and radius BA. Can you complete the last seven steps of the construction?

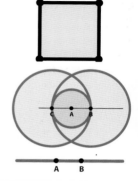

HINT: The next step is to find the third corner of the square point C, right above A.

252. EUCLID C

DRAW a regular hexagon (all sides and all angles the same) using only a straightedge and compass. Here is a method from *The Elements*.
1. Given two points A and B, use the straightedge to draw segment AB.
2–3. Use the compass to draw a circle with center A and radius AB, and another circle with center B and radius BA. Can you complete the last seven steps of the construction?

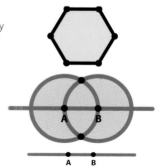

HINT: You already have four corners of the hexagon. How can you find the other two?

WHAT COMMON THEME connects all three of these images? The answer may involve wordplay.

HINT: hot stuff

FILL EACH GRID so every row, column, and colored region contains one of each number 1 to 6. Each marked diagonal must also contain one of each number 1 to 6.

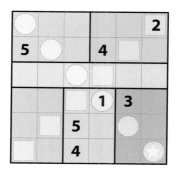

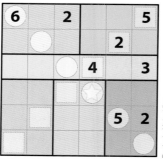

Puzzles by Michael Rios

HINT: In the top puzzle, the star must be a 5 because this is the only place a 5 can appear in the descending diagonal. In the bottom puzzle, the star must be a 2 because this is the only place a 2 can appear in the descending diagonal.

255. DOT MATRIX

HOW MANY dots will be in the next figure in the sequence below?

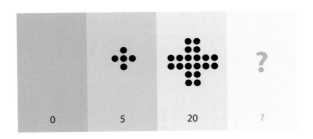

0   5   20   ?

HINT: The cross is always made of five squares of dots.

256. MISTRANSLATION

THESE TITLES of classic movies were translated by a computer to another language, then back into English, with surprising results. What were the original titles?

ANGRY GRAPE (1940)

INSIDE RAIN SONG (1952)

IT GOES WITH WIND (1939)

SOME APPRECIATE IT WARMTH (1959)

HINT: John Ford, Gene Kelly, George Cukor, Billy Wilder

WHICH TWO patterns look the same when folded into cubes?

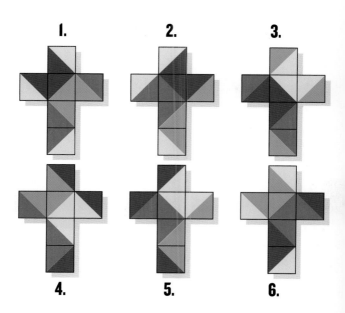

I.

2.

3.

4.

5.

6.

HINT: Pattern 1 is not one of the two matching patterns.

WHAT COMMON THEME connects all three of these images? The answer may involve wordplay.

HINT : king of, baseball, ring

EXPLAIN why the sequence

1 2 2 3 3 4...

could be logically continued as any of the following:

A **...4 5 5 6 6 7 7 8 8**

B **...4 4 5 5 5 6 6 6 6**

C **...5 6 6 7 7 8 9 10 10**

For instance, the sequence 1 2 1 2 3
could be continued as the expanding sequence
(1 2) (1 2 3) (1 2 3 4) (1 2 3 4 5)...
or as the paired sequence
(1 2) (1 2) (3 4) (3 4) (5 6) (5 6)...

HINT: Group the second sequence as (1) (2 2) (3 3) (4 4 4) (5 5 5) (6 6 6 6)...

260. DOT MATRIX

PUZZLE TYPE: NUMBER	DIFFICULTY: ✿
COMPLETION: ☐	TIME: _____

HOW MANY dots will be in the next figure in the sequence below?

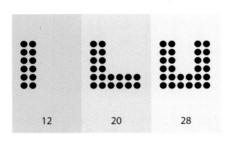

| 12 | 20 | 28 | ? |

HINT: Visualize the final figure and count the missing dots.

261. READ ME

PUZZLE TYPE: WORD	DIFFICULTY: ✿
COMPLETION: ☐	TIME: _____

DECODE these two familiar terms.

HINT: water words—initiate borrowing, everything but

THE BLUE PATH visits letters in the order MEAZ. Draw a path from start to end that visits letters in the order MAZE. You may not enter a square more than once.

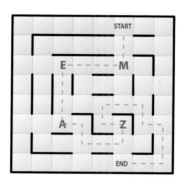

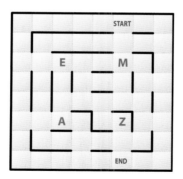

HINT: Approach the M from the right and the A from the left.

WHAT COMMON THEME
connects all three
of these images?
The answer may
involve wordplay.

HINT: turn for the better

EACH LETTER in the sum stands for a different digit. For instance, E equals 8. Can you find the values of the other letters? If a letter appears more than once, it always stands for the same digit. The first digit of a number is never 0. Use logic to deduce digits: Why must C equal 9?

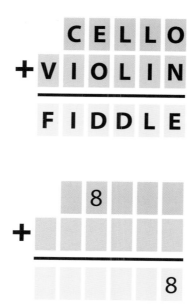

$$
\begin{array}{r}
\text{CELLO} \\
+\ \text{VIOLIN} \\
\hline
\text{FIDDLE}
\end{array}
$$

HINT: C must equal 9 because in the ten thousands place, C+1=I, which means C must be 0 or 9. But CELLO cannot start with a 0.

HOW MANY dots will be in the next figure in the sequence below?

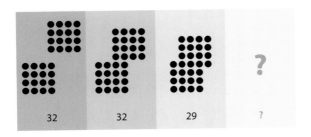

HINT: In what direction is the upper square moving from figure to figure?

DEDUCE the secret five-letter word from the clues. For instance, WRITE shares three letter tiles with RIGHT.

The secret word

shares three tiles with

B E G U N

and shares three tiles with

M I X U P

HINT: The secret word starts with the letter I.

WHICH SHAPES below can be made by rotating and overlapping the two pieces at right? You may not flip pieces over.

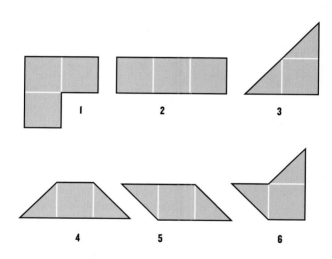

1

2

3

4

5

6

HINT: Of the six shapes, three cannot be made.

MATCH each garbled sentence with the type of error it contains. These examples were collected by cognitive scientists Douglas Hofstadter and David Moser. Hofstadter and Moser have written papers on how speech errors reveal how we think about language.

1. I have a lot of irons in the fire but I'm holding them close to my chest.

2. I won't comment—I won't take eitherbody's side.

3. It is kisstomary to cuss the bride.

4. This park covers the entire gambit of ages, young to old.

5. What they were saying was such small talk.

6. You have to either (a) have a job or (b) independently wealthy.

7. You hit the nail right on the nose.

MALAPROPISM: Replacing a word with a similar-sounding but inappropriate word. Example: "My wife and I took our kids to visit a wildlife refugee."

SPOONERISM: Switching the initial sounds of two words. Example: "Foon and spork."

MIXED METAPHOR: Combining two unrelated metaphors that are incompatible. Example: "No matter which fork in the road we take, it's not going to be clear sailing."

MALAPHOR: Splicing together two closely related figures of speech. Example: "She really stuck her neck out on a limb."

CANNIBALISM: One word "eating" part of the next word. Example: "He's wearing an MIT shirt."

GREASY SPOONERISM: Inappropriately modifying or calling out part of an indivisible stock phrase. Example: "Paul has a very sweet tooth."

PRODUCTIVE ERROR: Inventing a word that extends an existing pattern in language. Example: "I guess there's a power outage or something that is unabling her to answer."

HINT: Sentence 7 is a malaphor.

269. GIBBERISH B

PUZZLE TYPE: WORD	DIFFICULTY: ✿
COMPLETION: ☐	TIME: _____

EACH of the following phrases is a common scientific term with two sounds swapped. Ignore spelling and pay attention only to sound. For instance, "shun sign" is a scrambled version of "sunshine."

1. Shun sign
2. Coarse mode
3. Fair oil
4. Lead of spite
5. Lumber nine

6. Mentor of sass
7. Tech wrangle
8. Toe preen
9. Walk shave
10. Wine save

HINT: Phrase 2 is Morse code.

270. GIBBERISH C

PUZZLE TYPE: WORD	DIFFICULTY: ✿✿✿
COMPLETION: ☐	TIME: _____

EACH of the sentences below, when spoken aloud, sounds like a more sensible utterance. Can you decode the gibberish?

1. How to wreck a nice beach you sing calm incense.
(Title of a paper about speech recognition.)

2. Un petit d'un petit, S'étonne aux Halles. (First line of a poem from Mots d'Heures: Gousses, Rames by Luis d'Antin Van Rooten. Despite appearances, the poem and book title are in English.)

3. Ladle Rat Rotten Hut. Wants pawn term, dare worsted ladle gull hoe lift wetter murder inner ladle cordage, honor itch offer lodge dock florist. (The beginning of a well-known tale, from the book *Anguish Languish* by H. L. Chace.)

HINT: Sentence 1 is "How to recognize speech using common sense," which is the name of a paper by Henry Lieberman on computer-aided speech recognition.

WHICH TWO figures match perfectly? Figures may be rotated.

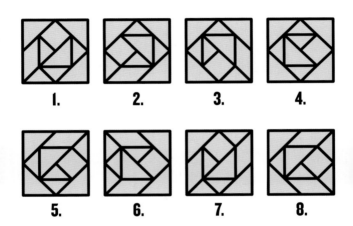

1.

2.

3.

4.

5.

6.

7.

8.

HINT: The two matching figures do not include figure 7 or figure 8.

272. BOOKSHELF

| PUZZLE TYPE: LOGIC | DIFFICULTY: ✸ |
| COMPLETION: ☐ | TIME: _____ |

REARRANGE the order of the books so the second letter of each title is the first letter of the next title. The second letter of the last title can be anything.

HINT: If BRAKES (book 2) is not last, it must be followed by ROUND (book 4).

273. DOT MATRIX

| PUZZLE TYPE: NUMBER | DIFFICULTY: ✸✸ |
| COMPLETION: ☐ | TIME: _____ |

HOW MANY dots will be in the next figure in the sequence below?

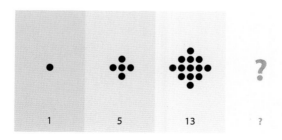

| 1 | 5 | 13 | ? |

HINT: What must you add to each figure to get the next figure?

PUZZLE TYPE: WORD
COMPLETION: ☐

DIFFICULTY: ✲✲
TIME: ______

IN THIS CROSSWORD each letter reads in two directions. Copy letters from the alphabet at top into the empty boxes. You may rotate and flip letters. Each word reads in the direction of its clue. The first letter is given.

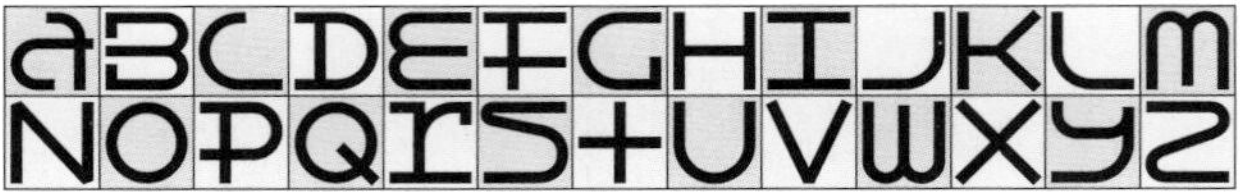

ABCDEFGHIJKLM
NOPQRSTUVWXYZ

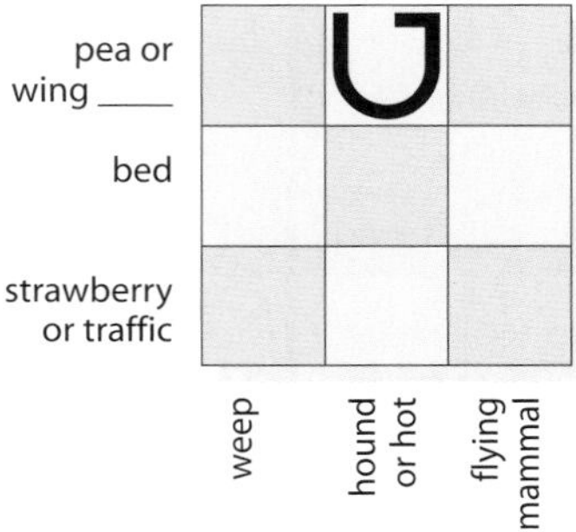

pea or wing ____
bed
strawberry or traffic
weep
hound or hot
flying mammal

HINT: The answer to "pea or wing" is "nut."

LAY SIX SHEETS of stationery flat on a table so three sheets overlap exactly one other sheet above and one below, and three sheets overlap exactly two other sheets above and two below. Sheets may not be folded, cut, or bent.

HINT: The solution has triangular symmetry.

WHICH TWO figures match perfectly?

1.   **2.**   **3.**   **4.**

5.   **6.**   **7.**   **8.**

HINT: The two matching figures do not include figure 3 or figure 4.

HOW do the figures on the left differ from the figures on the right?

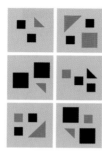
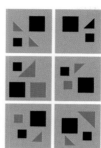

HINT: size comparison

HOW MANY dots will be in the next figure in the sequence below?

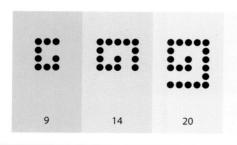

9   14   20   ?

HINT: Visualize the next figure and count the missing dots.

FIND 28 words spelled forward or backward, straight or diagonal, that combine with BOX to make a common word or phrase. The leftover letters spell a relevant quotation and its author.

V	I	R	T	S	P	R	I	N	G	U	E
L	H	H	A	D	N	A	S	E	A	T	S
E	I	S	T	S	M	U	I	O	K	O	W
T	N	R	A	H	S	A	F	N	I	P	E
T	B	W	A	C	O	G	I	F	T	S	R
E	L	O	O	T	U	R	T	L	E	D	B
R	O	O	O	A	N	U	I	S	W	T	N
R	Y	H	F	M	D	G	N	O	R	T	S
I	O	D	S	F	B	O	D	A	E	R	B
E	X	O	N	F	I	A	E	P	A	F	I
R	E	T	T	A	H	C	R	C	C	E	M
A	E	W	E	S	C	G	E	A	R	S	T

HINT: One of the longest words is "chatter."

MATCH EACH DETAIL with a different letter. For instance, detail 5 is from the T. All details are right side up and magnified the same amount.

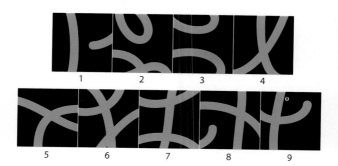

5	___	___	___	___	___	___	___

HINT: Detail 6 is from the N.

WHICH TWO figures match perfectly? Figures may be rotated.

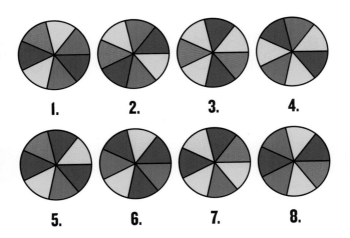

1.   2.   3.   4.

5.   6.   7.   8.

HINT: The two matching figures do not include figure 3 or figure 4.

282. BY ANALOGY

EACH EQUATION below uses the same rule to combine letters of two words to make a third word. Figure out the rule, then fill in the missing word.

TEAS + **SEAT** = **EAST**

EROS + **ROES** = **ROSE**

SNAP + **SPAN** = **NAPS**

STAR + **ARTS** =

HINT: Watch for red herrings.

283. DOT MATRIX

HOW MANY dots will be in the next figure in the sequence?

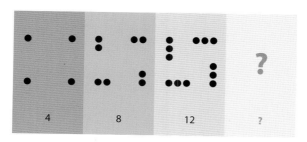

4   8   12   ?

HINT: What dots must you add to each figure to make the next figure?

WRITE A LETTER in each bubble to spell words that fit the clues. The first word has been given. Then rearrange all the letters in gold bubbles to make a word that ends with COM.

com Ⓔ move closer

com ◯◯ pause punctuation

com ◯◯◯ fight, war

com ◯◯◯◯ put together, merge

com ◯◯◯◯◯ professional laugh getter

com ◯◯◯◯◯◯ military chief

com ◯◯◯◯◯◯ settlement with concessions

com ◯◯◯◯◯◯◯ exchange information

◯◯◯◯◯◯◯◯ device for talking in a building

HINT: From top to bottom, the gold bubbles contain the letters E, M, T, I, N, R, O, C.

| PUZZLE TYPE: SPATIAL | DIFFICULTY: ☀ |
| COMPLETION: ☐ | TIME: _____ |

THESE THREE people are making three linked rings. What surprising thing happens if one person withdraws from the assembly while the other two do not move?

Photo by Steve Dibartolomeo

HARRY AND HERMIONE, in *Harry Potter and the Sorcerer's Stone*, must escape a chamber by walking through a wall of flames. A row of seven unmarked, single-serving bottles, all of different sizes, sits on a table. The only way they can pass through safely is to choose the correct two bottles, and drink them. They read a poem listing five clues:

a. One bottle, which we will call F, contains a potion that will let you walk through the fire in front. Another bottle (B) contains a potion that will let you walk through the fire in back. Two bottles (W) contain wine that does nothing, and the remaining three bottles (P) contain poison.

b. Each wine bottle (W) has a poison bottle (P) immediately to its left.

c. The end bottles contain different liquids, and neither is F.

d. The biggest and smallest bottles are not poison (P).

e. The bottles second from each end contain the same liquid.

Looking at the bottles, Hermione concludes that the rightmost bottle is B, and the smallest bottle is F. Without seeing the bottles, what can you say about the location of the F bottle?

HINT: There are only eight arrangements of PPPWWBF that meet all these conditions. The book does not give us enough information to figure out which one of these arrangements was correct, but we do know that it must have been one of these eight. Figure out the eight arrangements and this puzzle gets much easier to solve.

LOOKING AT THE BOTTLES, Hermione concludes that the rightmost bottle is B, and the smallest bottle is F. Given that Hermione was able to solve the puzzle, what can you say about the positions of the smallest and biggest bottles?

HINT: Remember, rule d states that the biggest and smallest bottles are not poison (P).

IF THE POEM had not mentioned clue d about biggest and smallest bottles, which bottle could Hermione have chosen knowing she would not be poisoned if she drank it?

If the biggest and smallest bottles had been in positions 1 and 4, what would Hermione have done?

HINT: List all the possible solutions (there aren't very many). Which bottle is safe in all possible solutions?
If the biggest and smallest bottles are in positions 1 and 4, respectively, there are just two possible solutions.

FIND where each detail appears in the big picture.

Photo by © istock.com / Matthew Maude

I   2   3   4   5   6

HINT: Detail 1 is in the middle left.

FILL EACH GRID so every row, column, and colored region contains one of each number 1 to 6.

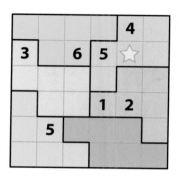

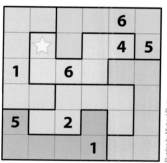

Puzzles by Michael Rios

291. DOT MATRIX

| PUZZLE TYPE: NUMBER | DIFFICULTY: ❀ |
| COMPLETION: ☐ | TIME: _____ |

FIGURE OUT how the dot patterns change from one frame to the next. What will the final frame look like, and how many dots will it contain?

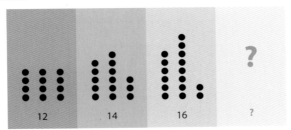

12   14   16   ?

HINT: Consider one column at a time. How does the number of dots in the first column change from one frame to the next? What about the other columns?

292. OUT OF ORDER

| PUZZLE TYPE: WORD | DIFFICULTY: ❀❀❀ |
| COMPLETION: ☐ | TIME: _____ |

UNSCRAMBLE the letters in each word pair to make two new related words. All pairs follow the same theme.

DARK BOG = _____ + _____

COW MEAT = _____ + _____

ASHES SINK = _____ + _____

BRANDY YOKE = _____ + _____

HINT: Animal talk. The words in the first pair start with D and B.

HOW MANY triangles of any size can you find in the figure? To get you started, one triangle has been outlined.

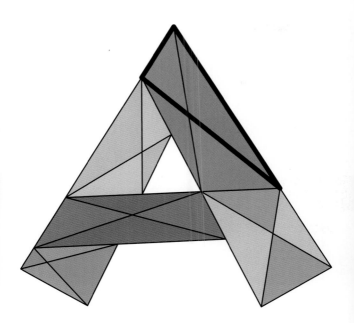

HINT: Be sure to find all the triangles that encircle the triangular hole.

FIND where each detail appears in the big picture.

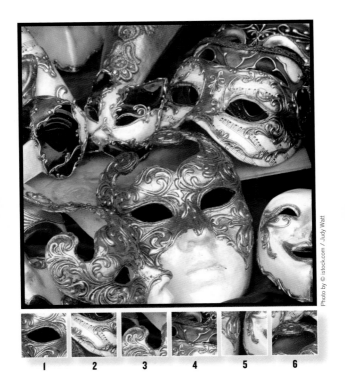

Photo by © istock.com / Judy Watt

1   2   3   4   5   6

HINT: Detail 1 is in the lower middle.

HOW do the letters on the left differ from the letters on the right?

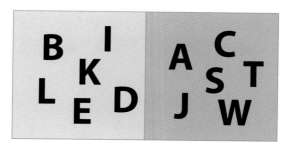

HINT: Imagine holding the letter with your right hand and feeling it with your left.

FIGURE OUT how the dot patterns change from one frame to the next. What will the final frame look like, and how many dots will it contain?

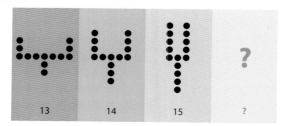

13   14   15   ?

HINT: The answer is not 16 dots.

DECODE these two familiar terms.

HINT: Size matters—how it all started, Disney song.

THE BLUE PATH visits letters in the order BANAAN. Draw a path from start to end that visits letters in the order BANANA. You may not enter a square more than once.

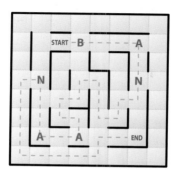

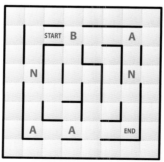

HINT: Go right to B, then A. Then go to the N on the left.

| PUZZLE TYPE: VISUAL | DIFFICULTY: ✿ ✿ ✿ |
| COMPLETION: ☐ | TIME: _____ |

FIND where each detail appears in the big picture.

Photo © istock.com / Radu Razvan

1   2   3   4   5   6

HINT: Detail 1 is in the middle left.

ABE AND BARB sat with one chair between them. So did Carl and Deb. Ed sat farther forward than Abe, Barb, or Carl. Where did Fay sit?

HINT: Where could Ed sit if he was farther forward than three other people?

PUZZLE TYPE: NUMBER	DIFFICULTY: ☀
COMPLETION: ☐	TIME: _____

FIGURE OUT how the dot patterns change from one frame to the next. What will the final frame look like, and how many dots will it contain?

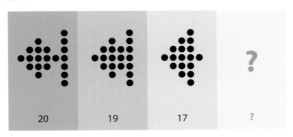

20   19   17   ?

HINT: What two shapes are moving through each other?

PUZZLE TYPE: WORD	DIFFICULTY: ☀☀☀
COMPLETION: ☐	TIME: _____

DEDUCE the secret five-letter word from the clues. For instance, WRITE shares three letter tiles with RIGHT.

The secret word

☐ ☐ ☐ ☐ ☐

shares three tiles with

B O W E D

and shares no tiles with

H O U S E

HINT: The secret word starts with the letter B.

WHICH SHAPES below can be made by
rotating and overlapping the two pieces
at right? You may not flip pieces over.

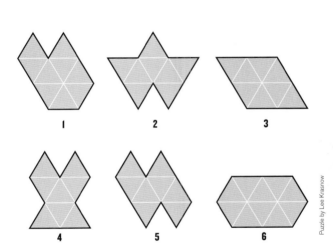

1

2

3

4

5

6

Puzzle by Lee Krasnow

HINT: Of the six shapes, three cannot be made.

IN HER BOOK *King of Infinite Space* (Walker & Company, 2006), author Siobhan Roberts tells the story of Donald Coxeter, a geometer whose 80 years of productive work inspired many such figures as mathematician John Conway, inventor Buckminster Fuller, and artist M. C. Escher. Coxeter was a strong advocate of geometry in education, writing that "the ability to visualize geometrically is a basic part of the scientist's mental equipment." Here is a teaser Coxeter used to excite his students' geometric imaginations.

Slice an apple in half, not from top to bottom as conventionally done, but across the equator. What symmetry do you see in the middle?

HINT: This symmetry also appears in many plants and animals, including starfish, sand dollars, and apple flowers.

PUZZLE TYPE: SPATIAL
COMPLETION: ☐

DIFFICULTY: ✿✿
TIME: _____

TIE A STRIP of paper in an overhand knot, pull it tight without crumpling the paper, and flatten it. What shape do you get? Can you predict the result before you do it?

HINT: The strip will be folded over to change direction three times.

306. SHAPE UP C

PUZZLE TYPE: SPATIAL
COMPLETION: ☐

DIFFICULTY: ✿✿✿
TIME: _____

SLICE a cube of cheese in half, not parallel to a face, but by balancing the cube on one corner and slicing across the equator parallel to the ground. What shape is the resulting cross-section?

HINT: The cut passes through parts of all six faces of the cube.

WHAT COMMON THEME connects all three of these images? The answer may involve wordplay.

HINT: be nimble

308. BOOKSHELF

| PUZZLE TYPE: LOGIC | DIFFICULTY: ✿ ✿ |
| COMPLETION: ☐ | TIME: _____ |

REARRANGE the books so adjacent book titles never contain the same letter. Make the leftmost number as low as possible.

BEND 1 HALT 2 HANG 3 MASK 4 SLED 5 TYPE 6

HINT: HALT (book 2) can only be next to BEND (book 1).

309. SPARE CHANGE

| PUZZLE TYPE: NUMBER | DIFFICULTY: ✿ ✿ |
| COMPLETION: ☐ | TIME: _____ |

WHAT is the largest amount of postage you cannot make exactly with 4- and 7-cent stamps?

HINT: The answer is between 10 and 20 cents.

THESE WELL-KNOWN SAYINGS were translated by computer to another language, then back into English, with surprising results. What were the original figures of speech?

Rear of 8 spheres.

Rests in the switch.

The short extremity of the pole.

Penny-intelligently and lbs stupidly.

HINT: in a tough spot, inattentive, shafted, shortsighted

PUZZLE TYPE: SPATIAL	DIFFICULTY: ✹✹
COMPLETION: ☐	TIME: _____

MATCH EACH DETAIL with a different letter. For instance, detail 5 is from the D. All details are right side up and magnified the same amount.

DYNAMITE

5

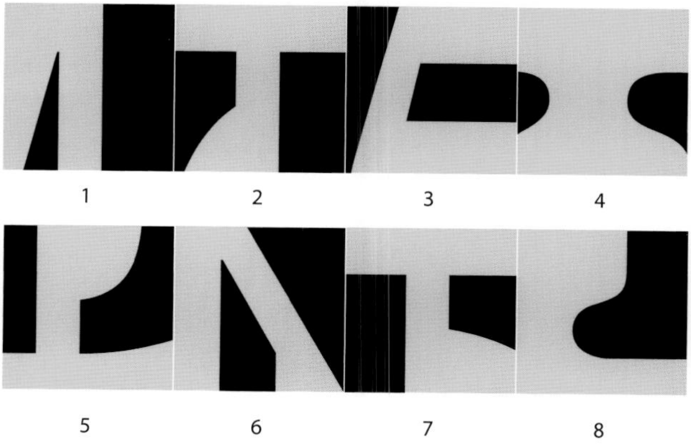

1   2   3   4

5   6   7   8

HINT: Detail 6 is from the N.

WHAT COMMON THEME connects all three of these images? The answer may involve wordplay.

HINT: do re mi fa so la ti do

HOW do the figures on the left differ from the figures on the right?

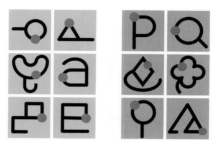

HINT: Each body has a tail and a dot.

FIND three different ways to make exact change for 50 cents using exactly 10 coins. Your change may include pennies, nickels, dimes, and quarters.

HINT: All the solutions include at least one nickel.

315. WORD SEARCH

| PUZZLE TYPE: WORD | DIFFICULTY: ✿ ✿ ✿ |
| COMPLETION: ☐ | TIME: _____ |

FIND 32 words spelled forward or backward, straight or diagonal, that combine with FISH to make a common word or phrase. The leftover letters spell a relevant quotation.

M	A	K	K	N	G	Y	S	A	I	L	G
G	O	J	L	N	F	W	I	R	S	I	H
I	O	E	U	I	O	N	K	G	A	A	W
I	F	L	Y	R	M	M	C	T	P	T	H
O	E	L	D	E	E	N	O	B	I	U	S
T	K	Y	A	T	S	L	R	N	P	T	O
W	I	L	I	T	R	I	G	G	E	R	B
N	G	H	P	U	I	N	L	N	T	I	L
S	W	O	L	B	W	E	F	V	A	L	U
I	N	O	W	S	I	A	N	G	E	L	E
D	H	K	O	T	F	H	R	H	E	R	Y
A	R	E	B	A	E	F	S	C	T	E	R

MAKING a circle with your fingers is easy. Can you make each of the shapes below with just your thumbs and forefingers?

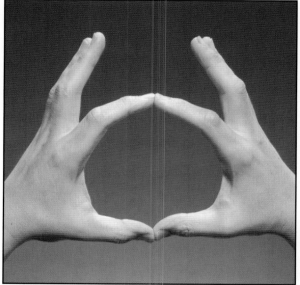

Photo by Steve Savage

HINT: Thumbs do not have to touch thumbs.

WHAT COMMON THEME
connects all three
of these images?
The answer may
involve wordplay.

HINT: bind together

EACH EQUATION below uses the same rule to combine letters of two words to make a third word. Figure out the rule, then fill in the missing word.

TIED + ITEM = TIDE

CUP + URN = UP

SHOW + TOW = TWO

USE + MAGIC =

HINT: First run the two words together.

WHAT is the most change you can have and not be able to make exact change for a dollar? Your change may include pennies, nickels, dimes, and quarters.

HINT: The answer is a little more than $1.

WRITE A LETTER in each bubble to spell words that fit the clues. The first word has been given. Then rearrange all the letters in the gold bubbles to make a word that ends with CAR.

car **E** concern, affection
car ○○ cut material to make a shape
car ○○○ floor covering
car ○○○○ related to the heart
car ○○○○○ merry-go-round
car ○○○○○○ sideways gymnastic move
car ○○○○○○○ bubbly, as in a soda
car ○○○○○○○○ meat-eating
car ○○○○○○○○○ edible starch

○○○○○○○○○ local train

HINT: From top to bottom, the gold bubbles contain the letters E, T, C, S, T, A, R, R.

HOW MANY pentagons of any size can you find in the figure? To get you started, one pentagon has been outlined.

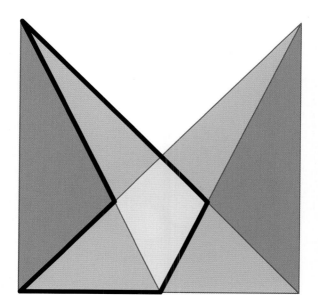

HINT: A pentagon is a polygon with five sides. The sides don't have to be the same length. All of the pentagons in this figure are concave, meaning one of the corners points inward.

EACH day of the week, the trendy Combinatorial Café challenges diners to create their own three-item combination plates from nine à la carte items on the menu, shown below.

1. Monday's monothematic plate is three different items that are either all the same color or all the same shape. How many different combination plates are possible?

2. Tuesday's panchromatic plate is any three different items of three different colors. How many different combination plates are possible?

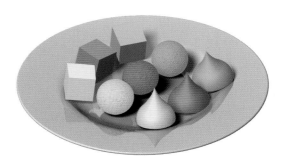

1. Wednesday's triadic plate is any three different items. How many different combination plates are possible?

2. Thursday's metamorphic plate is three different items that include at least two different shapes. How many different combination plates are possible?

HINT: 1. First pick any one of the nine items. Then choose any one of the remaining eight items. 2. Which combinations are forbidden?

1. Friday's binary plate is any three different items that include just two colors and two shapes. How many combination plates are possible?

2. The weekend's mix master plate is any three items, no two of which are the same color or the same shape. How many different combination plates are possible?

HINT: 1. Omit one color and one shape and you are left with four items to choose from. 2. The answer is less than 10.

WHICH TWO figures match perfectly?

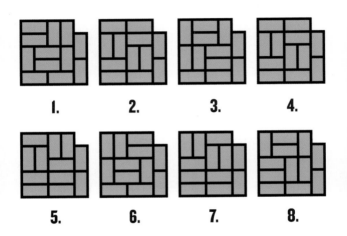

1.   2.   3.   4.

5.   6.   7.   8.

HINT: The two matching figures do not include figure 5 or figure 6.

FILL EACH GRID so every row, column, and colored region contains one of each number 1 to 6. Each marked diagonal must also contain one of each number 1 to 6.

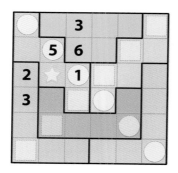

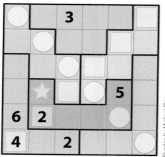

Puzzles by Michael Rios

327. SPARE CHANGE

WHAT is the largest amount of postage you cannot make exactly with 5- and 8-cent stamps?

HINT: The answer is between 25 and 50 cents.

328. MISTRANSLATION

THESE TITLES were translated by a computer to another language, then back into English, with surprising results. What were the original titles? All are in the 200 top-grossing U.S. movies.

UPPER RIFLE (1986)

REGULATE THE FRAUD (1994)

INTERCEPT ME, IF THEM ABILITY (2002)

THE INTRUDER OF THE REFUGE WHICH IS GONE (1981)

HINT: Cruise, Schwarzenegger, DiCaprio, Ford

THE PATH through the green maze makes exactly 20 turns, each marked with a blue square. Can you draw a maze on the yellow board with a single path from start to end through every square, making just 14 turns? You must use the red line as a wall.

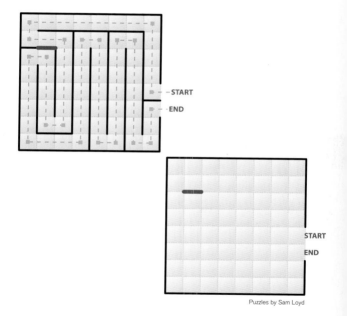

Puzzles by Sam Loyd

WHICH TWO figures match perfectly? Figures may be rotated.

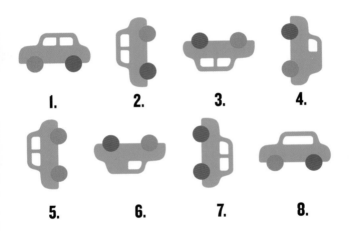

1.　　**2.**　　**3.**　　**4.**

5.　　**6.**　　**7.**　　**8.**

HINT: The two matching figures do not include figure 7 or figure 8.

331. SEEK WHENCE

PUZZLE TYPE: LOGIC
COMPLETION: ☐
DIFFICULTY: ✹✹✹
TIME: ______

EXPLAIN why the sequence

1 1 2 3 3 5...

could be logically continued as any of the following:

A ...5 5 8 7 7 11 9 9 14

B ...4 7 5 9 6 11 7 13 8

C ...7 7 10 13 13 17 21 21

For instance, the sequence **1 2 1 2 3**
could be continued as the expanding sequence
(1 2) (1 2 3) (1 2 3 4) (1 2 3 4 5) . . .
or as the paired sequence
(1 2) (1 2) (3 4) (3 4) (5 6) (5 6) . . .

HINT: Group the first sequence as (1 1) 2 (3 3) 5 (5 5) 8 (7 7) 11 (9 9) 14 . . .

FIND two different ways to make exact change for 30 cents that use exactly the same number of coins.

HINT: Don't use any dimes.

DECODE these two familiar phrases.

HINT: shapely sayings—faulty logic, interrogation

WHICH SHAPES below can be made by rotating and overlapping the two pieces at right? You may not flip pieces over.

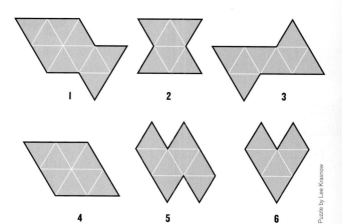

1

2

3

4

5

6

Puzzle by Lee Krasnow

HINT: Of the six shapes, two cannot be made.

WHICH TWO figures match perfectly? Figures may be rotated.

1.

2.

3.

4.

5.

6.

7.

8.

HINT: The two matching figures do not include figure 5 or figure 6.

EACH LETTER in the sum stands for a different digit. For instance, N equals 6. Can you find the values of the other letters? If a letter appears more than once, it always stands for the same digit. The first digit of a number is never 0. Use logic to deduce digits: Why must H equal 4?

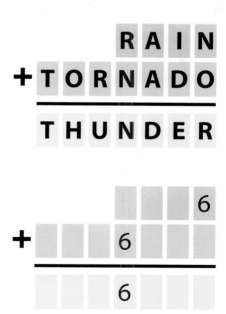

337. SPARE CHANGE

| PUZZLE TYPE: NUMBER | DIFFICULTY: ✹✹ |
| COMPLETION: ☐ | TIME: _____ |

WHAT is the most money you can have in $1, $2, $5, $10, $20, and $50 bills and not be able to make exact change for a $100 bill?

HINT: The answer is more than $100 but less than $150.

338. SECRET WORD

| PUZZLE TYPE: WORD | DIFFICULTY: ✹✹✹✹ |
| COMPLETION: ☐ | TIME: _____ |

DEDUCE the secret five-letter word from the clues. For instance, WRITE shares three letter tiles with RIGHT.

The secret word

☐ ☐ ☐ ☐ ☐

shares three tiles with

B O U T S

and shares three tiles with

W H I S K

HINT: The secret word starts with the letter H.

MATCH EACH DETAIL with a different letter. For instance, detail 3 is from the J. All details are right side up and magnified the same amount.

HINT: Detail 7 is from the U.

| PUZZLE TYPE: SPATIAL | DIFFICULTY: ✿✿ |
| COMPLETION: ☐ | TIME: _____ |

THE BODY stores instructions for making a human being in DNA, a long molecule coiled in a compact tangle that consists of a sequence of base pairs: the nucleotides adenine, cytosine, guanine, and thymine. These nucleotides act like symbols in an alphabet. The matrix shown below has just two symbols, ⬤ and ◯, packed in a 10 x 15 grid. These symbols form twisted paths through the matrix. Travel from the green start dot to any of the dots in the bottom row by following a path formed by the repeating pattern ⬤ ⬤ ⬤ ◯ . . . You may move only left, right, up, or down (not diagonally) from one symbol to the next. The first few steps are given.

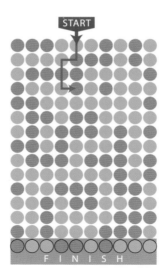

START

FINISH

HINT: The next three steps are right, right, up.

THE MATRIX shown at right has just two symbols, 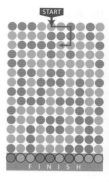 and ⬤, packed in a 10 x 15 grid. These symbols form twisted paths through the matrix. Find the shortest possible path from the green start dot in the top row to any of the dots in the bottom row that follows the repeating pattern ⬤⬤⬤⬤⬤⬤⬤⬤ ...
You may move only left, right, up, or down (not diagonally). The first few steps are given.

HINT: The next three steps are left, down, down.

THE MATRIX shown at right has just two symbols, 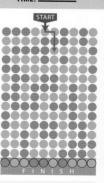 and ⬤, packed in a 10 x 15 grid. These symbols form twisted paths through the matrix. Find the shortest possible path from the green start dot in the top row to any of the dots in the bottom row that follows the repeating pattern ⬤⬤⬤⬤⬤⬤ ... You may move only left, right, up, or down (not diagonally). The first few steps are given.

HINT: The next three steps are down, right, down.

FIND where each detail appears in the big picture.

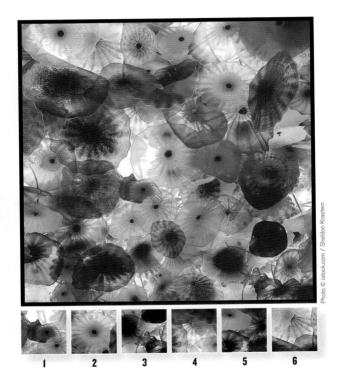

Photo © istock.com / Sheldon Krastein

1   **2**   **3**   **4**   **5**   **6**

HINT: Detail 1 is in the lower middle.

344. BOOKSHELF

| PUZZLE TYPE: LOGIC | DIFFICULTY: ☀ |
| COMPLETION: ☐ | TIME: _____ |

REARRANGE the books so the name of each book is the number on the next book. The last book can have any name.

HINT: Book 6 must come first because it is not the title of any other book.

345. SPARE CHANGE

| PUZZLE TYPE: NUMBER | DIFFICULTY: ☀ ☀ |
| COMPLETION: ☐ | TIME: _____ |

I HAVE some dimes in my left hand. I have some combination of nickels and quarters in my right hand. The number of coins in each hand is the same, as is the total value of the coins in each hand. What is the smallest possible total value of the money in each hand?

HINT: The total number of coins in both hands is less than 12.

| PUZZLE TYPE: WORD | DIFFICULTY: ✿ ✿ ✿ |
| COMPLETION: ☐ | TIME: _____ |

IN THIS CROSSWORD each letter reads in two directions. Copy letters from the alphabet at top into the empty boxes. You may rotate and flip letters. Each word reads in the direction of its clue. The first letter is given.

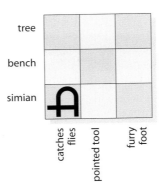

tree

bench

simian

catches flies

pointed tool

furry foot

MAKING two linked loops with your fingers is easy. Can you make a knotted loop like the one shown with just your thumbs and forefingers?

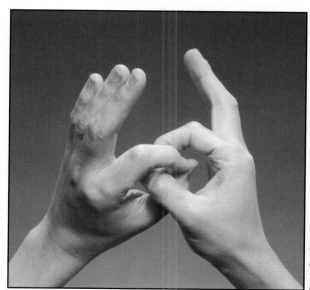

Photo by Steve Dibartolomeo

HINT: Your hands can face toward you or away from you.

FIND where each detail appears in the big picture.

Photo © istock.com / Vera Bogaer

1   2   3   4   5   6

HINT: Detail 1 is in the upper middle right.

HOW do the figures on the left differ from the figures on the right?

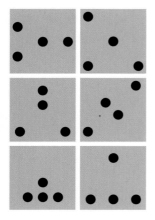
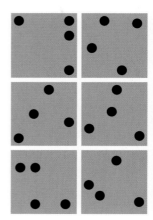

WHAT is the largest amount of change you can have and not be able to make exact change for a dollar if you have coins worth 1, 2, 5, 10, 20, 25, and 50 cents?

HINT: The answer is more than $1.50.

HOW MANY L shapes can you find in the figure at right? The L shapes must have exactly the same proportions as the outlined example, but can be any size, rotated or flipped over.

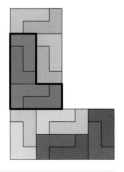

HINT: The L shapes come in three sizes.

FIND 29 words spelled forward or backward, straight or diagonal, that combine with BED to make a word or phrase. For instance, COBWEB + BED = COBWEBBED. The leftover letters spell a relevant quotation.

N	E	L	L	S	N	U	B	P	O	S	T
V	E	I	B	B	A	L	B	R	R	H	G
O	V	N	U	N	E	D	D	I	R	T	O
E	F	E	L	L	O	W	V	O	T	M	B
H	M	N	F	S	E	E	B	U	R	C	S
P	O	S	T	E	R	W	C	O	U	D	M
A	O	B	M	H	A	A	F	Y	C	D	H
S	R	A	N	T	N	T	S	S	K	G	T
A	R	Y	E	O	A	B	H	T	I	B	U
F	O	R	P	L	B	P	I	E	A	O	A
N	A	Y	P	C	D	F	L	R	R	N	I
G	D	A	E	R	P	S	H	T	C	K	D

HINT: The longest word is "platform."

PUZZLE TYPE: **VISUAL**	DIFFICULTY: ☼
COMPLETION: ☐	TIME: _____

FIND where each detail appears in the big picture.

Photo © istockphoto.com / Nathan Borror

1 2 3 4 5 6

HINT: Detail 1 is in the middle.

| PUZZLE TYPE: LOGIC | DIFFICULTY: ✿ ✿ ✿ |
| COMPLETION: ☐ | TIME: _____ |

EACH EQUATION below uses the same rule to combine letters of two words to make a third word. Figure out the rule, then fill in the missing word.

RISE + DOOR = STEP

CANE + DIRT = DOES

SITE + FORT = TUGS

PITY + HUSK =

HINT: Think alphabetically.

355. SPARE CHANGE

| PUZZLE TYPE: NUMBER | DIFFICULTY: ✿ ✿ ✿ |
| COMPLETION: ☐ | TIME: _____ |

WHAT is the largest amount of postage you cannot make exactly with 7- and 11-cent stamps?

HINT: The answer is between 50 cents and $1.00.

WRITE A LETTER in each bubble to spell words that fit the clues. The first word is given. Then rearrange all the letters in the gold bubbles to make a word that begins with INC.

inc Ⓘ Ⓣ Ⓔ cause, stir up
inc ◯◯◯ paycheck, money received
inc ◯◯◯◯ moving along slowly
inc ◯◯◯◯ sharp tooth
inc ◯◯◯◯◯ sit on an egg
inc ◯◯◯◯◯◯ motivation, encourages action
inc ◯◯◯◯◯◯◯ prone to starting a fire
inc ◯◯◯◯◯◯◯ out of place, odd
inc ◯◯◯◯◯◯◯◯ radiating light

◯◯◯◯◯◯◯◯◯ undercover

HINT: From top to bottom, the gold bubbles contain the letters I, O, I, O, T, N, N, G, C.

PUZZLE TYPE: SPATIAL	DIFFICULTY: ✿✿✿
COMPLETION: ☐	TIME: _____

THE PATH through the green maze makes exactly 19 turns. Can you draw a maze with a single path from start to end through every square, making the maximum possible number of right-angle turns? You must use the red line as a wall.

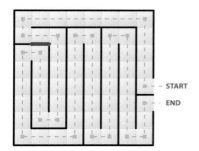

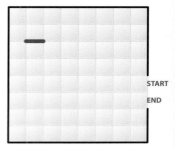

358. GEO SCRAMBLE A

PUZZLE TYPE: WORD
COMPLETION: ☐

DIFFICULTY: ✲✲✲
TIME: ________

REARRANGE each phrase to make a word from geometry.

1. alarm galloper
2. barley hop
3. earth rodent
4. grey tin motor

HINT: 1. rickety rectangle, 2. two-part cousin of the parabola, 3. solid shape with four faces, 4. mathematics of triangles

| PUZZLE TYPE: WORD | DIFFICULTY: ✿✿✿ |
| COMPLETION: ☐ | TIME: _____ |

REARRANGE each phrase to make a word from geometry.

> ## 1. hop dearly
> ## 2. nuclear dipper
> ## 3. prime tree
> ## 4. read time

HINT: 1. three-dimensional shapes, 2. right angular, 3. outside edge, 4. across the middle of a circle

| PUZZLE TYPE: WORD | DIFFICULTY: ✿✿✿ |
| COMPLETION: ☐ | TIME: _____ |

REARRANGE each phrase to make a word from geometry.

> ## 1. relate quail
> ## 2. sees coils
> ## 3. to scribe
> ## 4. upset honey

HINT: 1. all edges same length, 2. two edges same length, 3. cuts a line or angle in half, 4. diagonal side of a right triangle

WHAT COMMON THEME connects all three of these images? The answer may involve wordplay.

HINT: Well, hello.

FILL EACH grid so every row, column, and colored region contains one of each number 1 to 6.

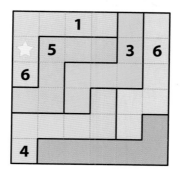

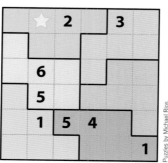

Puzzles by Michael Rios

WHAT is the largest amount of change you can have and not be able to make exact change for a dollar if you have coins worth 1, 2, 3, 5, 10, 20, 25, and 50 cents?

HINT: The answer is more than $2.00.

UNSCRAMBLE the letters in each word pair to make two new related words. All pairs follow the same theme.

UNLACE NUT = _____ + _____

SOUTH GARDEN = _____ + _____

SHORTER TRIBES = _____ + _____

HAT THEREFROM = _____ + _____

HINT: All in the family. The words in the first pair start with A and U.

PUT together three of these pieces to make a square. You may rotate pieces, but not flip them to make their mirror images.

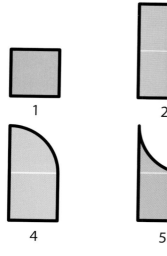

1

2

3

4

5

6

HINT: The square has dimensions 2 by 2.

WHAT COMMON THEME
connects all three
of these images?
The answer may
involve wordplay.

HINT: something that goes back and forth

367. CATEGORIES

HOW do the letters on the left differ from the letters on the right?

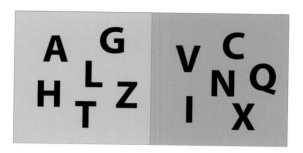

HINT: Draw the letters and watch how your hand moves.

368. SPARE CHANGE

I HAVE some nickels in my left hand. I have some combination of pennies and dimes in my right hand. The number of coins in each hand is the same, as is the total value of the coins in each hand. What is the smallest possible total value of the money in each hand?

HINT: The total value of the coins in my left hand is less than 50 cents.

DECODE these two familiar terms.

HINT: mainstream, almost crazy

MATCH EACH DETAIL with a different letter. For instance, detail 6 is from the E. All details are right side up and magnified the same amount.

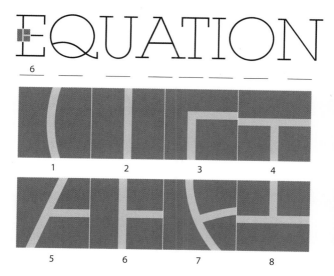

HINT: Detail 7 is from the Q.

WHAT COMMON THEME connects all three of these images? The answer may involve wordplay.

HINT: count

ABE AND BARB sat in different rows and columns. So did Carl and Deb. So did Ed and Fay. Abe sat just in front of Ed, and Barb sat just left of someone else other than Ed. Where did Fay sit?

373. SPARE CHANGE

I HAVE some dimes in my left hand. I have some combination of pennies and quarters in my right hand. The number of coins in each hand is the same, as is the total value of the coins in each hand. What is the smallest possible total value of the money in each hand?

HINT: The total value of the coins in my left hand is more than 50 cents.

374. SECRET WORD

DEDUCE the secret five-letter word from the clues. For instance, WRITE shares three letter tiles with RIGHT.

The secret word

☐ ☐ ☐ ☐ ☐

shares three tiles with

A W F U L

and shares no tiles with

F A N C Y

HINT: The secret word starts with the letter W.

PUT your right hand in front of a mirror and you will see a left hand. Why does a mirror reverse left and right, not top and bottom?

Photo by Steve Savage

HINT: What if the mirror lies flat on the floor?

A DIAGONAL is a line joining two nonadjacent corners of a polygon. The hexagon is sliced into four triangles by three diagonals that do not cross one another. How many different ways are there to dissect this hexagon into triangles, using only noncrossing diagonals? Dissections that differ by rotation or reflection are considered different. For instance, the hexagon rotated by 60 degrees or 120 degrees would constitute a different dissection.

HINT: Be sure to include the dissections that contain an equilateral triangle.

AN ISOSCELES triangle is a triangle that has two sides the same length. (An equilateral triangle, which has all three sides the same length, also counts as an isosceles triangle because it, too, has two sides the same length.) The pentagon below has been dissected into three isosceles triangles, using only noncrossing diagonals. Can you dissect the hexagon and the octagon into isosceles triangles, using only noncrossing diagonals?

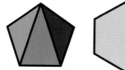
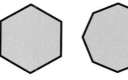

HINT: Remember that an equilateral triangle counts as an isosceles triangle.

THE PENTAGON below has been dissected into three isosceles triangles, using only noncrossing diagonals. Can you dissect a 12-sided polygon into isosceles triangles, using only noncrossing diagonals? Can you imagine how to do the same for a 24-gon or a 48-gon? How about a 64-gon or an 80-gon?

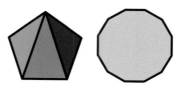

HINT: Notice that 12 is twice 6, and 24 is twice 12.

WHICH TWO figures match perfectly?

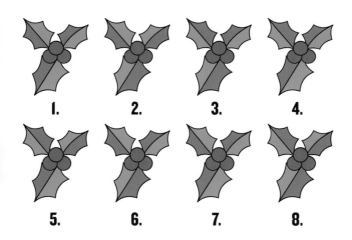

1.   **2.**   **3.**   **4.**

5.   **6.**   **7.**   **8.**

HINT: The two matching figures do not include figure 3 or figure 4.

| PUZZLE TYPE: LOGIC | DIFFICULTY: ✿✿ |
| COMPLETION: ☐ | TIME: _____ |

REARRANGE the books so adjacent book titles have at least one letter in common. The first book title is SCREAM.

HINT: The last book is BOO.

381. PATHOLOGY

| PUZZLE TYPE: NUMBER | DIFFICULTY: ✿ |
| COMPLETION: ☐ | TIME: _____ |

HOW MANY different paths get the car home? Go the right way on one-way roads (arrows), and do not visit any dot more than once. At right are two sample paths.

HINT: There are two roads from one dot to the next, and three chances to make a choice.

THESE WELL-KNOWN sayings were translated by a computer to another language, then back into English, with surprising results. What were the original figures of speech?

A shovel calls a shovel.

Do not form bones over it.

Throw to beads before pigs.

What it surrounds comes around.

HINT: honestly, candidly, wasted effort, karma

HOW MANY squares of any size and at any angle can you find in the figure? To get you started, two squares in black have been outlined. The red parallelogram does not count as a square.

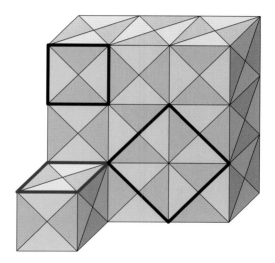

HINT: Turn the page 45 degrees to see the diagonal squares more clearly. Some squares use lines that appear to be on planes that are not parallel to the front surface.

THE LITTLE BOOK OF BIG MIND BENDERS   **299**

WHICH TWO figures match perfectly? Figures may be rotated.

1.

2.

3.

4.

5.

6.

7.

8.

HINT: The two matching figures do not include figure 3 or figure 4.

300 THE LITTLE BOOK OF BIG MIND BENDERS

PUZZLE TYPE: LOGIC	DIFFICULTY: ✹ ✹
COMPLETION: ☐	TIME: _____

HOW do the figures on the left differ from the figures on the right?

HINT: Play the angles.

IF YOU MULTIPLY the ages of my three kids, you get 36. If you add their ages, what is the smallest possible sum you might get?

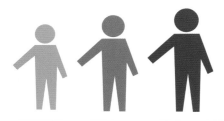

HINT: For instance, the three ages 1, 4, and 9 multiply to 36 and add to 14.

THE GREEN path visits letters in the order EAZM. Draw a path from start to end that visits letters in the order MAZE. You may not enter a square more than once.

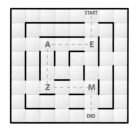

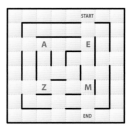

HINT: Approach the M from the bottom.

FIND 11 words spelled forward or backward, straight or diagonal, that combine with COUNTER to make a common word or phrase. The leftover letters spell a relevant quotation.

HINT: One of the longest words is "intuitive."

WHICH TWO figures match perfectly?

1.　　**2.**　　**3.**　　**4.**

5.　　**6.**　　**7.**　　**8.**

HINT: The two matching figures do not include figure 1 or figure 2.

PUZZLE TYPE: LOGIC
COMPLETION: ☐
DIFFICULTY: ✹✹✹
TIME: _____

EACH EQUATION below uses the same rule to combine letters of two words to make a third word. Figure out the rule, then fill in the missing word.

TEAS + EATS = EAST

EVEN + ROES = ROSE

TEN + TEEN = TENT

DUAL + KILN =

HINT: Look at the second word first.

391. PATHOLOGY

PUZZLE TYPE: NUMBER
COMPLETION: ☐
DIFFICULTY: ✹✹
TIME: _____

HOW MANY different paths get the car home? Go the right way on one-way roads (arrows), and do not visit any dot more than once. At right are two sample paths.

HINT: Each path must choose among two roads, then three roads, then four.

WRITE A LETTER in each bubble to spell words that fit the clues.
I've given you the first word. Then rearrange all the letters in the
gold bubbles to make a word that ends with RES.

res **T** relax, nap
res ⚪⚪ what you do to a clock after power loss
res ⚪⚪⚪ save from danger
res ⚪⚪⚪⚪ say again, in other words
res ⚪⚪⚪⚪⚪ someone who lives here
res ⚪⚪⚪⚪⚪⚪ artificial lake, water supply
res ⚪⚪⚪⚪⚪⚪⚪ place where people eat
res ⚪⚪⚪⚪⚪⚪⚪⚪ bring back to life
res ⚪⚪⚪⚪⚪⚪⚪⚪⚪ doubts, concerns

⚪⚪⚪⚪⚪⚪⚪⚪⚪ valuable things

HINT: From top to bottom, the gold bubbles contain the letters T, E, U, A, E, R, R, S, S.

PUT together three of these pieces to make a square. You may rotate pieces, but not flip them to make their mirror images.

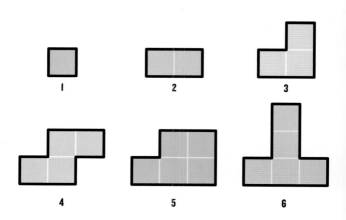

1

2

3

4

5

6

HINT: The square has dimensions 3 x 3.

TWO COUPLES, the Whites and the Blacks, dine together every Sunday, seated around a table with four chairs. To keep things fresh they like to switch chairs.

1. How many weeks can they dine together and sit in a different seating arrangement each time?

2. At the beginning of the meal they make a toast. If everyone clinks glasses with everyone else, how many clinks are there altogether?

HINT: Imagine seating the four people in order, one at a time. How many chairs can the first person choose among? How about the second person?

PUZZLE TYPE: NUMBER **DIFFICULTY:** ✹✹
COMPLETION: ☐ **TIME:** _____

TWO COUPLES, the Whites and the Blacks, have dinner together every Sunday, seated around a table with four chairs.

1. How many weeks can they have dinner together in different combinations if the members of each couple always sit across from each other?
2. How many weeks can they have dinner together in different seating arrangements if the members of each couple always sit next to each other?

HINT: The Whites can occupy either the north and south chairs, or the east and west chairs. Once the Whites are seated, there are two ways for the Blacks to sit.

PUZZLE TYPE: NUMBER **DIFFICULTY:** ✹✹✹
COMPLETION: ☐ **TIME:** _____

THREE COUPLES, the Whites, the Blacks, and the Grays, have dinner together every Sunday, seated around a table with six chairs.

1. How many weeks can they have dinner together in different combinations if the members of each couple always sit across from each other?
2. How many weeks can they have dinner together in different seating arrangements if the members of each couple always sit next to each other?

HINT: There are three pairs of opposite chairs. How many ways can the three couples be assigned to the three chair pairs?

PUZZLE TYPE: VISUAL
COMPLETION: ☐
DIFFICULTY: ✿✿
TIME: _____

FIND where each detail appears in the big picture.

Photo © istock.com / Rene Lee

1   2   3   4   5   6

HINT: Detail 1 is along the bottom.

PUZZLE TYPE: LOGIC	DIFFICULTY: ✿✿✿
COMPLETION: ☐	TIME: _____

FILL EACH GRID so every row, column, and colored region contains one of each number 1 to 6. The marked diagonal must also contain one of each number 1 to 6.

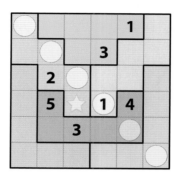

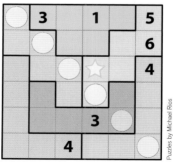

Puzzles by Michael Rios

399. PATHOLOGY

HOW MANY different paths get the car home? Go the right way on one-way roads (arrows), and do not visit any dot more than once. At right are two sample paths.

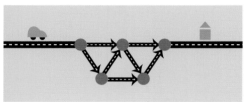

HINT: At each dot you can go straight or diagonal.

400. MISTRANSLATION

THESE TITLES were translated by a computer to another language, then back into English, with surprising results. What were the original titles? All are in the 200 top-grossing U.S. movies.

RETURNS FORWARD (1985)

THE RECHARGED TABLE (2003)

INDIVIDUAL OF SPIDERS (2002)

IT REPORTS SMALL AMOUNT (2002)

HINT: Zemeckis, Wachowski, Raimi, Spielberg

| PUZZLE TYPE: SPATIAL | DIFFICULTY: ✿ ✿ |
| COMPLETION: ☐ | TIME: _____ |

MAKE a five-pointed star using two fingers of one hand and two mirrors.

Photo by Steve DiBartolomeo

HINT: Stand the mirrors at an angle, hinged like a book.

FIND where each detail appears in the big picture.

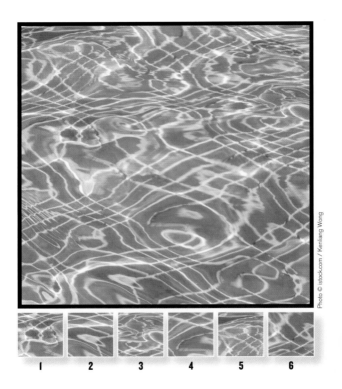

Photo © istock.com / Kenliang Wong

| 1 | 2 | 3 | 4 | 5 | 6 |

HINT: Detail 1 is in the middle left.

403. SEEK WHENCE

PUZZLE TYPE: LOGIC
COMPLETION: ☐
DIFFICULTY: ✹✹
TIME: ________

EXPLAIN why the sequence

1 2 1 2 3 2...

could be logically continued as any of the following:

A ...3 4 3 4 5 4 5 6 5 6

B ...3 2 5 2 5 2 7 2 7 2

C ...1 2 3 4 3 2 1 2 3 4

For instance, the sequence **1 2 1 2 3**
could be continued as the expanding sequence
(1 2) (1 2 3) (1 2 3 4) (1 2 3 4 5) . . . .
or as the paired sequence
(1 2) (1 2) (3 4) (3 4) (5 6) (5 6) . . . .

HINT: Group the first sequence as (1 2 1) (2 3 2) (3 4 3) (4 5 4) (5 6 5) (6 . . .)

404. PATHOLOGY

HOW MANY different paths get the car home?
Go the right way on one-way roads (arrows),
and do not visit any dot more than once. At right
are two sample paths.

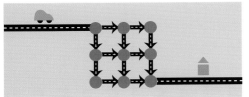

HINT: Each path uses a different combination of two vertical roads.

405. READ ME

DECODE these two familiar terms.

HINT: laugh again, available contract

| PUZZLE TYPE: SPATIAL
| COMPLETION: ☐

DIFFICULTY: ✿✿
TIME: _____

HOW MANY squares of any size can you find in the figure? To get you started, one square has been outlined in black.

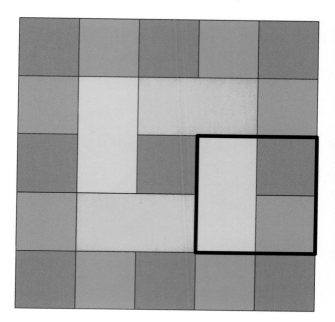

HINT: First count all the 1×1 squares, then all the 2×2, etc.

PUZZLE TYPE: VISUAL	DIFFICULTY: ✿ ✿ ✿
COMPLETION: ☐	TIME: _____

FIND where each detail appears in the big picture.

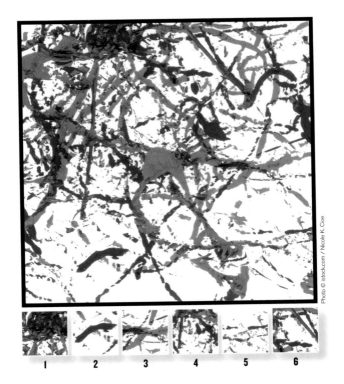

Photo © istockphoto.com / Nicole K. Cioe

1   2   3   4   5   6

HINT: Detail 1 is along the top.

| PUZZLE TYPE: | LOGIC |
| COMPLETION: ☐ | |

DIFFICULTY: ✿✿
TIME: _____

EACH LETTER in the sum stands for a different digit. For instance, S equals 6. Can you find the values of the other letters? If a letter appears more than once, it always stands for the same digit. The first digit of a number is never 0. Use logic to deduce digits: Why must R equal 9?

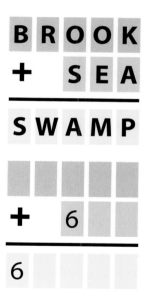

409. PATHOLOGY

PUZZLE TYPE: NUMBER
COMPLETION: ☐

DIFFICULTY: ✹✹
TIME: _____

HOW MANY different paths get the car home?
Go the right way on one-way roads (arrows), and
do not visit any dot more than once. Blue roads
are two-way. At right are two sample paths.

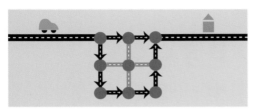

HINT: First count paths that move only left to right. Then include right-to-left roads.

410. SECRET WORD

PUZZLE TYPE: WORD
COMPLETION: ☐

DIFFICULTY: ✹✹
TIME: _____

DEDUCE the secret five-letter
word from the clues. For
instance, WRITE shares three
letter tiles with RIGHT.

The secret word

☐ ☐ ☐ ☐ ☐

shares three tiles with

E M P T Y

and shares four tiles with

T I N G E

HINT: The secret word starts with the letter I.

THE GREEN path visits letters in the order ANCANC. Draw a path from start to end that visits letters in the order CANCAN. You may not enter a square more than once. There is more than one solution.

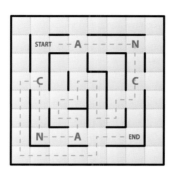

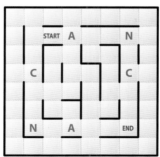

IN THE MOVIE *2001*, the intelligent computer HAL plays chess with astronaut Dave Bowman. The scene was also filmed with HAL playing a game with pentominoes—the 12 different shapes that can be formed by joining five squares edge to edge, as shown below. In the game, two players alternately place pentominoes from a complete set of 12 pieces on a chessboard. The first player who cannot place a piece without overlapping another piece loses. Every pentominoes game must end in 12 moves or less because there are only 12 pieces. The shortest possible game on an 8 × 8 board ends in just five moves. Here is the position after the first four moves. Can you play just one more piece so the other player cannot move? Remember, each piece can be played only once.

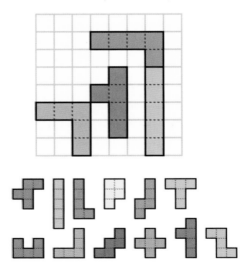

HINT: The pieces on the board create a narrow corridor of space. Which pentomino not on the board can fit somewhere in this space? That will be the piece that you play next.

322 THE LITTLE BOOK OF **BIG MIND BENDERS**

PUZZLE TYPE: SPATIAL
COMPLETION: ☐
DIFFICULTY: ✦✦✦✦
TIME: _____

CAN you place three pentominoes on a 6 × 6 board so no more pentominoes can be placed? Can you find two such solutions that use completely different pieces? Can you place four pentominoes on a 7 × 7 board so no more pentominoes can be placed? Can you find a solution where no pentomino touches the edge of the board?

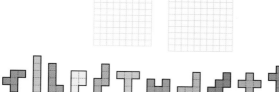

HINT: The key is to put pieces on the board so the only pieces that fit in the empty space are already on the board. For the 6 × 6 board, you can make the empty space be a narrow-row corridor or make empty spaces that are 2 × 3 rectangles.

PUZZLE TYPE: SPATIAL
COMPLETION: ☐
DIFFICULTY: ✦✦✦✦
TIME: _____

CAN you place six pentominoes on a 9 × 9 board so no more pentominoes can be placed? Can you place seven pentominoes on a 10 × 10 board so no more pentominoes can be placed?

HINT: The key is to put pieces on the board so the leftover space is cut into narrow strips.

WHAT COMMON THEME connects all three of these images? The answer may involve wordplay.

HINT: shape

| PUZZLE TYPE: LOGIC | DIFFICULTY: ✹✹ |
| COMPLETION: ☐ | TIME: _____ |

REARRANGE the books so the title of any book followed by the title of the next book always makes a five- or six-letter word.

HINT: COM comes first.

417. PATHOLOGY

| PUZZLE TYPE: NUMBER | DIFFICULTY: ✹✹ |
| COMPLETION: ☐ | TIME: _____ |

HOW MANY different paths get the car home? Go the right way on one-way roads (arrows), and do not visit any dot more than once. At right are two sample paths.

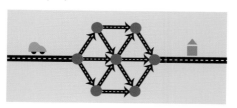

HINT: Count paths that stay in the upper half, then in the lower half, then in both.

IN THIS CROSSWORD each letter reads in two directions. Copy letters from the alphabet at top into the empty boxes. You may rotate and flip letters. Each word reads in the direction of its clue. The first letter is given.

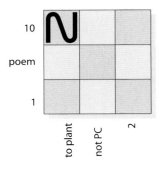

10

poem

1

to plant

not PC

2

HINT: The answer to "10" is "ten."

PUT together three of these pieces to make a square. You may rotate pieces, but not flip them to make their mirror images.

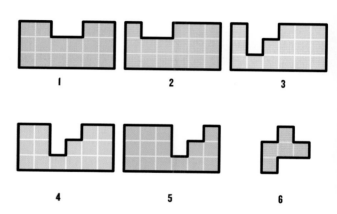

1

2

3

4

5

6

HINT: The square has dimensions 6 × 6.

WHAT COMMON THEME connects all three of these images? The answer may involve wordplay.

HINT: What type of piano?

HOW do the figures on the left differ from the figures on the right?

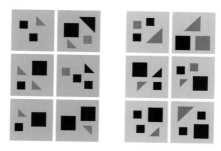

HOW MANY different paths get the car home? Go the right way on one-way roads (arrows), and do not visit any dot more than once. At right are two sample paths.

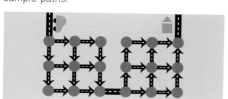

HINT: Count the number of paths through each half of the map, then multiply.

FIND 28 words spelled forward or backward, straight or diagonal, that combine with DOWN to make a common word or phrase. The leftover letters spell a relevant quotation.

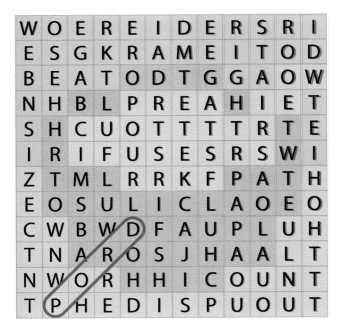

W	O	E	R	E	I	D	E	R	S	R	I
E	S	G	K	R	A	M	E	I	T	O	D
B	E	A	T	O	D	T	G	G	A	O	W
N	H	B	L	P	R	E	A	H	I	E	T
S	H	C	U	O	T	T	T	T	R	T	E
I	R	I	F	U	S	E	S	R	S	W	I
Z	T	M	L	R	R	K	F	P	A	T	H
E	O	S	U	L	I	C	L	A	O	E	O
C	W	B	W	D	F	A	U	P	L	U	H
T	N	A	R	O	S	J	H	A	A	L	T
N	W	O	R	H	H	I	C	O	U	N	T
T	P	H	E	D	I	S	P	U	O	U	T

HINT: The longest word is "comforter."

HANDSHAKES are normally for two people. Invent a handshake for three right hands. All three people must do exactly the same thing. Hands must touch, but need not grasp one another.

Photo by Steve Savage

HINT: There are many answers.

WHAT COMMON THEME connects all three of these images? The answer may involve wordplay.

HINT: Solar power may someday replace it.

FIGURE OUT at least two good answers for each alphabetic analogy.

1. ABC is to ABD as XYZ is to **WYZ**

2. AABC is to AABD as IJKK is to _____

3. ABC is to ABD as MRRJJJ is to _____

4. EFG is to DFG as GHI is to _____

HINT: What is similar about AABC and IJKK? What is different?

HOW MANY many different paths get the car home? Go the right way on one-way roads (arrows), and do not visit any dot more than once. Blue roads are two-way. At right are two sample paths.

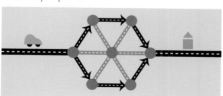

HINT: First count paths that move only left to right. Then include right-to-left roads.

WRITE A LETTER in each bubble to spell words that fit the clues. The first word is given. Then rearrange all the letters in the gold bubbles to make a word that ends with ALL.

all ⓞ ⓣ give a portion, dole out
all ◯◯◯ refer to, hint at
all ◯◯◯◯ fast tempo in music
all ◯◯◯◯◯ relating to silt left by a river
all ◯◯◯◯◯◯ union, e.g., between countries
all ◯◯◯◯◯◯◯ supposedly, said without proof
all ◯◯◯◯◯◯◯◯ 24-hour study session
all ◯◯◯◯◯◯◯◯◯ loyalties, e.g., to the flag
all ◯◯◯◯◯◯◯◯◯◯ pretty poetic pattern

◯◯◯◯◯◯◯◯◯ a way to fix software

HINT: From top to bottom, the gold bubbles contain the letters T, E, R, L, I, L, N, S, A.

HOW MANY squares of any size can you find in this colorful frame? To get you started, one square has been outlined in black.

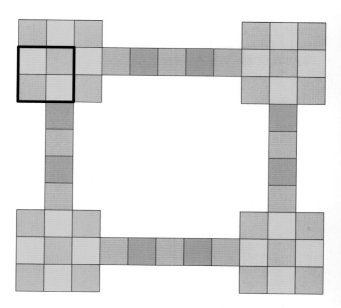

HINT: Don't forget the squares that encircle the big white hole.

IN THE MOVIE 2001, astronauts Poole and Bowman discuss turning off the intelligent computer HAL. They try to hide their words by talking in a soundproof chamber, but HAL reads their lips. Match each mouth animation below with one word of the following dialogue:

"I DON'T THINK WE'D HAVE ANY ALTERNATIVES. THERE ISN'T A SINGLE ASPECT OF SHIP OPERATIONS THAT'S NOT UNDER HIS CONTROL."

1. _____

2. _____

3. _____

HINT: To figure out the mouth positions for a word, break the word into a series of vowels and consonants, and notice what your lips and tongue do as you pronounce each sound. For instance, when you pronounce the TH of THINK, your mouth is partially open, somewhat narrow, with your tongue touching the roof of your mouth. 1. The first mouth position in word 1 is T of TH. 2. The second mouth position in word 2 is short I or short U. 3. The last mouth position in word 3 is R.

431. LIP READING B

MATCH each mouth animation below with one word of the following dialogue:

> "I DON'T THINK WE'D HAVE ANY ALTERNATIVES. THERE ISN'T A SINGLE ASPECT OF SHIP OPERATIONS THAT'S NOT UNDER HIS CONTROL. IF HE WERE PROVEN TO BE MALFUNCTIONING, I WOULDN'T SEE HOW WE'D HAVE ANY CHOICE BUT DISCONNECTION." "I'M AFRAID I AGREE . . ."

1. _____

2. _____

3. _____

HINT: 1. The first mouth position in word 1 is CH. 2. The third mouth position in word 2 is R. 3. The last mouth position in word 3 is L.

432. LIP READING C

PUZZLE TYPE: VISUAL
COMPLETION: ☐

DIFFICULTY: ✹✹
TIME: _____

MATCH each mouth animation below with one word of the dialogue shown in puzzle 431:

1. _____

2. _____

3. _____

HINT: 1. The last mouth position in word 1 is T or TH. 2. The last mouth position in word 2 is D or N. 3. The first mouth position in word 3 is M, B, or P.

WHICH TWO figures match perfectly? Figures may be rotated.

1.

2.

3.

4.

5.

6.

7.

8.

HINT: The two matching figures do not include figure 3 or figure 4.

EACH LETTER in the sum stands for a different digit. For instance, T equals 8. Can you find the values of the other letters? If a letter appears more than once, it always stands for the same digit. The first digit of a number is never 0. Use logic to deduce digits: Why must R equal 0 or 9?

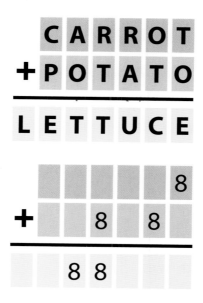

HINT: R must equal 0 or 9 because R + 8 = 8 in the thousands place. The letter O equals 6.

| PUZZLE TYPE: NUMBER | DIFFICULTY: ✿ ✿ ✿ |
| COMPLETION: ☐ | TIME: _____ |

HOW MANY different paths get the car home? Go the right way on one-way roads (arrows), and do not visit any dot more than once. At right are two sample paths.

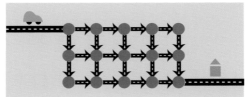

HINT: Each path uses a different combination of two vertical roads.

436. OUT OF ORDER

| PUZZLE TYPE: WORD | DIFFICULTY: ✿ ✿ ✿ |
| COMPLETION: ☐ | TIME: _____ |

UNSCRAMBLE the letters in each word pair to make two new related words. All pairs follow the same theme.

RIVER CARD = _____ + _____

ORDER HIRES = _____ + _____

RODEO BREAK = _____ + _____

SUPREME COURT = _____ + _____

HINT: Who's in charge? The words in the first pair start with C and D.

PUZZLE TYPE: SPATIAL	DIFFICULTY: ✸✸
COMPLETION: ☐	TIME: _____

DRAW a path from START to END, without going through walls, that visits all letters of HELIUM in any order. The path may not visit any square more than once. There are six different solutions.

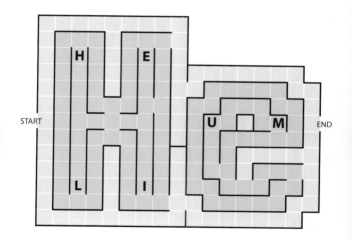

START

END

WHICH TWO figures match perfectly?

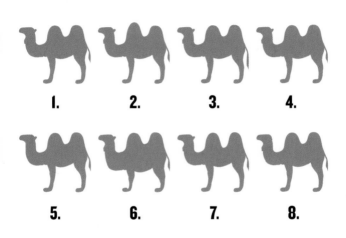

1.   **2.**   **3.**   **4.**

5.   **6.**   **7.**   **8.**

HINT: The two matching figures do not include figure 5 or figure 6.

EACH LETTER in the sum stands for a different digit. For instance, the letter I equals 8. Can you find the values of the other letters? If a letter appears more than once, it always stands for the same digit. Numbers never start with 0. Use logic to deduce digits. Why must N equal an even number?

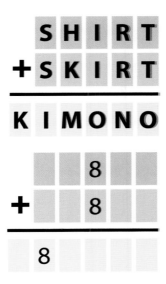

PUZZLE TYPE: NUMBER   **DIFFICULTY:** ✹✹✹
COMPLETION: ☐   **TIME:** _____

HOW MANY different paths get the car home? Go the right way on one-way roads (arrows), and do not visit any dot more than once. At right are two sample paths.

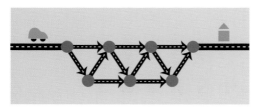

HINT: Start with the completely straight path, then systematically introduce diagonals.

---

441. READ ME

PUZZLE TYPE: WORD   **DIFFICULTY:** ✹✹
COMPLETION: ☐   **TIME:** _____

DECODE these two familiar terms.

HINT: Count those letters.

PUT together three of these pieces to make a square. You may rotate pieces, but not flip them to make their mirror images.

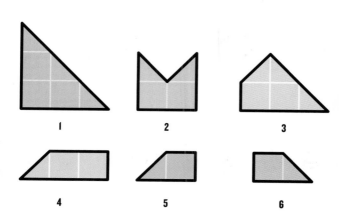

1

2

3

4

5

6

HINT: The square has dimensions 3 × 3.

WHICH TWO figures match perfectly?

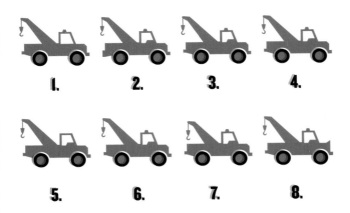

1.   2.   3.   4.

5.   6.   7.   8.

HINT: The two matching figures do not include figure 7 or figure 8.

EACH LETTER in the sum stands for a different digit. For instance, the letter O equals 4. Can you find the values of the other letters? If a letter appears more than once, it always stands for the same digit. Numbers never start with 0. Use logic to deduce digits: Why must U equal 0 or 9?

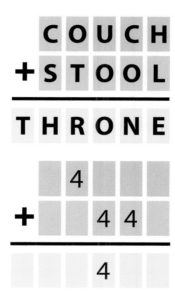

COUCH
+ STOOL
————————
THRONE

      4
+   4 4
————————
      4

HINT: U must equal 0 or 9 because U + 4 = 4 in the hundreds place. H equals 2.

HOW MANY different paths get the car home? Go the right way on one-way roads (arrows), and do not visit any dot more than once. Blue roads are two-way. At right are two sample paths.

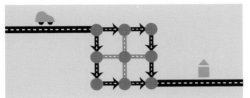

HINT: First count paths that move only left to right. Then include right-to-left roads.

DEDUCE the secret five-letter word from the clues. For instance, WRITE shares three letter tiles with RIGHT.

The secret word

shares no tiles with
B I R T H

and shares three tiles with
W I N C H

HINT: The secret word starts with the letter C.

| PUZZLE TYPE: SPATIAL | DIFFICULTY: ✿ ✿ ✿ |
| COMPLETION: ☐ | TIME: _____ |

MAKE a cube using the fingers of one hand and three mirrors.

Photo by Steve Savage

HINT: Place one mirror horizontally and stand the other two at a right angle.

ARTHUR C. CLARKE'S short story "The Sentinel," which inspired the movie *2001*, features an alien artifact shaped as a regular tetrahedron, a geometric form bounded by four equilateral triangles. For the movie, the artifact became a more visually impressive rectangular monolith. Clarke's story describes the monolith as having proportions 1 to 4 to 9, though the movie did not adhere to these numbers. Here is a challenge that relates the two monolith shapes: hexahedron (solid bounded by six quadrilaterals) and tetrahedron (solid bounded by four triangles).

1. Slice a 1 × 4 × 9 rectangular hexahedron to reveal an equilateral triangle cross-section.

2. Slice a regular tetrahedron to reveal a square cross-section.

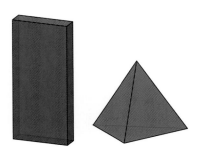

HINT: 1. A very small slice will suffice. **2.** Slicing a tetrahedron parallel to the ground reveals a triangle. To reveal a square, the slice must be at an angle.

1. Draw all six edges of a regular tetrahedron on the surface of a regular hexahedron (cube).

2. Draw all 12 edges of a hexahedron (not necessarily rectangular), that has two opposite faces that are 4 × 9 rectangles on the surface of a regular tetrahedron.

HINT: **1.** All the corners of the tetrahedron are also corners of the hexahedron. **2.** None of the corners of the hexahedron are corners of the tetrahedron.

1. Cut a rectangular hexahedron into five tetrahedra.

2. Cut a tetrahedron into four nonrectangular hexahedra.

HINT: **1.** Assuming the hexahedron is a cube, one of the tetrahedra will be a regular tetrahedron, and the others are not regular. **2.** The four hexahedra meet at a point in the center of the tetrahedron.

CAN you figure out why these 12 pentomino shapes are in this particular order? These shapes appear in puzzles #412, 413, and 414, pages 322–323.

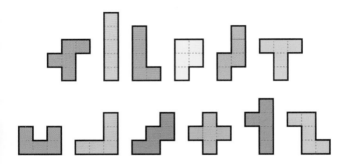

HINT: The last shape looks like the letter Z.

WHAT is the logic behind this sequence of four SHAPE COUNT diagrams? The first diagram appears in puzzle #406, page 317.

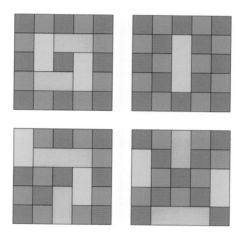

WHAT does this diagram have to do with this book?

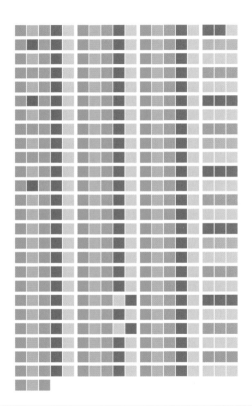

HINT: There are 453 squares in this diagram.

SOLUTIONS

#1 / DETAILS / PAGE 2

#2 / SUDOKU / PAGE 3

3	1	6	5	4	2
2	6	3	4	5	1
5	4	2	1	3	6
4	2	1	3	6	5
1	3	5	6	2	4
6	5	4	2	1	3

4	6	3	5	2	1
3	2	4	1	5	6
1	5	2	6	3	4
5	3	1	4	6	2
6	1	5	2	4	3
2	4	6	3	1	5

#3 / GO FIGURE / PAGE 4

The three ages are 1, 4, and 6, which multiply to 24 and add to 11.

#4 / OUT OF ORDER / PAGE 4

night vs. day; young vs. old; strong vs. weak; inside vs. outside

#5 / SHAPE COUNT / PAGE 5

16 one-by-one squares + 9 two-by-two squares + 4 three-by-three squares + 1 four-by-four square = 30 squares

#6 / THREE OF A KIND / PAGE 6

The theme is plates. License plate, tectonic plates, dinner plates.

#7 / CATEGORIES / PAGE 7

left: straight strokes
right: curved strokes

#8 / GO FIGURE / PAGE 7

The smallest possible sum is 10. You get the smallest sum when the ages are close together. The closest ages that multiply to 36 are 3, 3, and 4, which add to 10.

#9 / OUT OF ORDER / PAGE 8

new vs. old
true vs. false
over vs. under
opposite vs. similar

#10 / COVER STORY / PAGE 9

A TALE
OF TWO
CITIES
DAVID
COPPER
FIELD

#11 / PERFECT MATCH / PAGE 10

Figures 5 and 8 match perfectly.

5   8

#12 / WHO SAT WHERE? / PAGE 11

Fay sat in seat 6. Ed sat in seat 1, so Abe and Barb sat in seats 2 and 5. Carl and Deb sat in the middle row in seats 3 and 4, leaving just seat 6 for Fay.

#13 / GO FIGURE / PAGE 12

The three ages are 9, 2, and 2, which multiply to 36, and add to 13. The other set of ages that works is 6, 6, and 1, which also multiply to 36 and add to 13. Knowing that the oldest kid is at least a year older than the other kids eliminates the 6, 6, 1 solution, leaving only the 9, 2, 2 solution.

#14 / OUT OF ORDER / PAGE 12

soft vs. loud; hard vs. easy; black vs. white; broken vs. fixed

#15 / CUBE SQUARED / PAGE 13

Patterns 2 and 4 look the same when folded into cubes.

#16 / MIRROR WORDS / PAGE 14

1. ATOM
2. UTAH
3. TOY
4. OUTWIT
5. MYTH
6. AWAY
7. TOMATO

First letters spell AUTOMAT

#17 / **MIRROR WORDS** / PAGE 14

1. DODO
2. ECHO
3. CHECK
4. OBOE
5. DECIDE
6. EBBED
7. DIOXIDE
First letters spell DECODED

#18 / **TUMBLING** / PAGE 15

1. Red = 3, yellow = 1, blue = 9
2. Red = 3, yellow = 9, blue = 1
3. Red = 9, yellow = 1, blue = 3
4. Red = 1, yellow = 9, blue = 3
5. Red = 9, yellow = 3, blue = 1
6. Red = 1, yellow = 3, blue = 9

#19 / **DETAILS** / PAGE 16

#20 / **GRID LOGIC** / PAGE 17

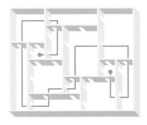

#21 / **GO FIGURE** / PAGE 17

Ben is 7 and Alex is 2, a difference of five years. In three years they will be 10 and 5, and 10 is twice 5.

#22 / **MISTRANSLATION** / PAGE 18

Silence is golden. Look before you leap. All roads lead to Rome. Better safe than sorry. What goes up must come down.

#23 / **MAZE** / PAGE 19

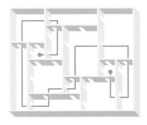

#24 / DETAILS / PAGE 20

#25 / CATEGORIES / PAGE 21

left: red dot covers a sharp corner; *right:* red dot covers a smooth line.

#26 / GO FIGURE / PAGE 21

Ben is 9 and Alex is 3, and 9 is three times 3. In three years they will be 12 and 6, and 12 is twice 6.

#27 / WORD SEARCH / PAGE 22

A verbal contract isn't worth the paper it's written on. —*Samuel Goldwyn*

#28 / MENTAL BLOCKS / PAGE 23

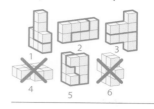

#29 / DETAILS / PAGE 24

#30 / BY ANALOGY / PAGE 25

#31 / GO FIGURE / PAGE 25

Ben is 8 and Alex is 2. Multiplying their ages gives you 16. In three years they will be 11 and 5, which also add to 16.

#32 / WORD LADDER / PAGE 26

#33 / PAPER WORK / PAGE 27

Arrange the six sheets in a single hexagonal loop, or in two triangular loops.

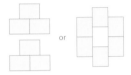

#34 / THE 15 PUZZLE A / PAGE 28

The solver put the blocks in the following order, turned the entire tray a quarter turn clockwise, then twisted each block back right side up. Note that the tray ends up in a different orientation.

4	8	12	
3	7	11	15
2	6	10	14
1	5	9	13

#35 / THE 15 PUZZLE B / PAGE 29

No matter how you move the blocks, the red 1 piece can never get past the barrier formed by the 2 and 3 blocks.

#36 / THE 15 PUZZLE C / PAGE 29

No matter how you move the pieces, the small blocks always stay in ascending order 1-2-3 reading clockwise around the big 4 block. The second tray has the small blocks in counterclockwise ascending order.

#37 / THREE OF A KIND / PAGE 30

Things that come in tens. Ten pins, ten commandments, ten fingers.

#38 / SUDOKU / PAGE 31

#39 / GO FIGURE / PAGE 32

Beth could have at most eight kids, ages 1, 2, 3, 4, 6, 8, 12, and 24.

#40 / MISTRANSLATION / PAGE 32

Star Wars. Rear Window. It Happened One Night. Guess Who's Coming to Dinner. (The hints are first names of lead actors.)

#41 / LETTER PARTS / PAGE 33

#42 / THREE OF A KIND / PAGE 34

Things that rhyme with "ox." Blocks, fox, clocks.

#43 / SEEK WHENCE / PAGE 35

a. (1 1 2) (1 1 2 3) (1 1 2 3 4) (1 1 . . .
   Sequences of increasing length that start 1 1 and count up.
b. (1) (1 2 1) (1 2 3 2 1) (1 2 3 4 3 . . .
   Sequences of increasing length that start at 1, count up, then back down to 1.
c. (1 1 2) (1 1 2) (1 1 2) (1 1 2) (1 1 . . .
   The sequence (1 1 2) repeating over and over.

This puzzle is based on the research project Seek Whence (a computer program that extrapolates numerical sequences), by cognitive scientist Douglas Hofstadter,

author of *Fluid Concepts and Creative Analogies.*

#44 / GO FIGURE / PAGE 36

Their ages are 6, 10, and 15. 2 divides evenly into 6 and 10, 3 divides evenly into 6 and 15, and 5 divides evenly into 10 and 15, but there is no number bigger than 1 that divides evenly into all three numbers 6, 10, and 15.

#45 / READ ME / PAGE 36

home stretch; homespun

#46 / BODY SHAPES / PAGE 37

Make one square with right hands, another with left hands. Move one hand to the other group to make a triangle and a pentagon.

#47 / THREE OF A KIND / PAGE 38

Things associated with Benjamin Franklin. *Poor Richard's Almanack* (written by Franklin), kite, bifocals (invented by Franklin).

#48 / ALPHAMETICS / PAGE 39

```
    8 5 2 8
+ 9 5 8 2 8
---------
1 0 4 3 5 6
```

#49 / GO FIGURE / PAGE 40

Bob could have at most six kids, ages 11, 13, 15, 17, 19, and one more who is either 14 or 16.

#50 / SECRET WORD / PAGE 40

ACHED

#51 / SHAPE COUNT / PAGE 41

From front layer to back there are 21 + 20 + 24 = 65 holes.

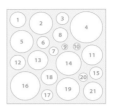

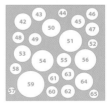

#52 / TETRIS A / PAGE 42

There are 39 possible landing positions. Note that in the real Tetris game you can rotate pieces as they fall, not just before they fall.

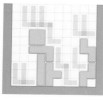

11

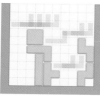

9

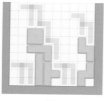

10

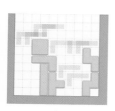

9

#53 / TETRIS B / PAGE 43

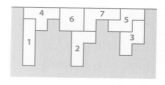

#54 / TETRIS C / PAGE 43

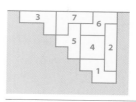

#55 / PERFECT MATCH / PAGE 44

Figures 1 and 7 match perfectly.

#56 / GRID LOGIC / PAGE 45

8 1 6
3 5 7
4 9 2

#57 / GO FIGURE / PAGE 45

Zane is 73 and Mabel is 37. Twice 37 is 74, which is just one more than 73.

#58 / CRAZY CROSS / PAGE 46

#59 / COVER STORY / PAGE 47

#60 / PERFECT MATCH / PAGE 48

Figures 2 and 8 match perfectly.

2   8

#61 / CATEGORIES / PAGE 49

left: each figure contains two dots that are near each other; *right:* no dots are near each other.

#62 / GO FIGURE / PAGE 49

Mabel is 1 and Zane is 6. Written side by side gives you 16. In 30 months they will be 4 and 8, which gives you 48, which is 3 times 16.

#63 / WORD SEARCH / PAGE 50

Freedom of the press is limited to those who own one.—*A. J. Liebling*

#64 / CUBE SQUARED / PAGE 51

Patterns 2 and 4 look the same when folded into cubes.

#65 / PERFECT MATCH / PAGE 52

Figures 2 and 4 match perfectly.

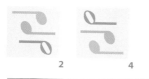

#66 / BY ANALOGY / PAGE 53

The first and last letters of both words combine to make the third word.

SEAT + AGAR = STAR

GAIN + ABET = GNAT

FOUR + ELSE = FREE

LOGO + CALK = LOCK

#67 / GO FIGURE / PAGE 53

Zane is 65 and Mabel is 59. On a calculator, 65 is the same as 59 turned upside down.

#68 / WORD LADDER / PAGE 54

#69 / MAZE / PAGE 55

One possible answer:

#70 / FAMILY MATH A / PAGE 56

The first player wins by taking one coin. From then on, if the second player takes one coin, the first player takes two coins, and if the second player takes two coins, the first player takes one coin. In either case, the number of coins is reduced by a total of three coins after two turns, and the first player always takes the last coin.

#71 / FAMILY MATH B / PAGE 56

The most number of crossings you can get with 5 pieces of spaghetti is 10, as shown. Notice that adding piece 5 adds four crossings—one for each time it crosses each of the previous pieces. Similarly, adding piece 6 adds five crossings, piece 7 adds six crossings, and so on. The total crossings are:
5 pieces = 10 crossings (6 + 4)
6 pieces = 15 crossings (10 + 5)
7 pieces = 21 crossings (15 + 6)
8 pieces = 28 crossings (21 + 7)

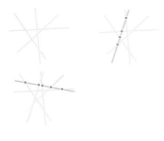

#72 / FAMILY MATH C / PAGE 57

The cards appear in the order ace, 3, 5, 7, 9, 2, 6, 10, 8, and 4.

#73 / DETAILS / PAGE 58

#74 / SUDOKU / PAGE 59

3	1	4	5	6	2
6	4	3	2	1	5
1	5	2	6	4	3
2	6	1	3	5	4
5	3	6	4	2	1
4	2	5	1	3	6

5	2	1	4	6	3
6	4	3	5	1	2
1	3	6	2	5	4
2	1	5	3	4	6
3	6	4	1	2	5
4	5	2	6	3	1

#75 / ASSEMBLIES / PAGE 60

There are eight ways to fit the pieces into the box, as shown below. There is one solution with no vertical pieces, four solutions with two vertical pieces, and three solutions with four vertical pieces.

#76 / OUT OF ORDER / PAGE 60

oil vs. water; early vs. late; past vs. future; zero vs. infinity

#77 / MENTAL BLOCKS / PAGE 61

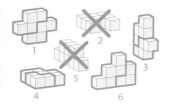

#78 / DETAILS / PAGE 62

#79 / CATEGORIES / PAGE 63

left: two strokes touch the baseline; *right:* one stroke touches.

#80 / ASSEMBLIES / PAGE 63

There are 12 ways to fit the pieces into the box, as shown below. There is one solution with all horizontal pieces, one with all vertical pieces, five with two vertical pieces, and five with four vertical pieces.

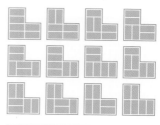

#81 / READ ME / PAGE 64

parallel universes; red shift

#82 / **PAPER WORK** / PAGE 65

Arrange the six sheets in two layers of triangles, one atop the other. Each sheet touches its two neighbors in the same layer, plus one sheet in the other layer.

#83 / **DETAILS** / PAGE 66

#84 / **WHO SAT WHERE?** / PAGE 67

Fay sat in seat 5. Abe and Barb sat in seats 1 and 6, Carl sat in seat 4 behind and one seat to the left of Deb in seat 2. Ed sat in seat 3, to the right of Deb, leaving seat 5 for Fay.

#85 / **ASSEMBLIES** / PAGE 68

There are eight ways to fit the pieces into the box, as shown below. There is one solution with zero vertical pieces, three with two vertical pieces, three with four vertical pieces, and one with six vertical pieces.

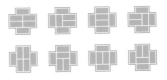

#86 / **SECRET WORD** / PAGE 68

ACUTE

#87 / **LETTER PARTS** / PAGE 69

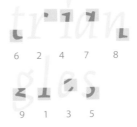

#88 / **TANGRAMS A** / PAGE 70

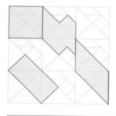

#89 / **TANGRAMS B** / PAGE 71

#90 / **TANGRAMS C** / PAGE 71

#91 / **THREE OF A KIND** / PAGE 72

Things designed for left-handed people: left-handed scissors (blades cross the other way), left-handed playing cards, left-handed watch (winding stem on left).

#92 / **GRID LOGIC** / PAGE 73

EYE
LOG
MUG

#93 / **ASSEMBLIES** / PAGE 73

There are 12 ways to fit the pieces into the box, as shown. The L piece can go in five places.

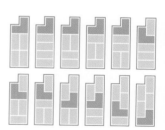

#94 / MISTRANSLATION / PAGE 74

Business before pleasure. Love is blind. As you sow, so shall you reap. Too many cooks spoil the broth. Let the buyer beware.

#95 / BODY SHAPES / PAGE 75

Each person joins their own thumbs together to make a straight edge. Everyone tips their left hand low and right hand high to make four vertical edges. Finally, everyone joins fingertips with their neighbors.

#96 / THREE OF A KIND / PAGE 76

Things that involve the word "stock." livestock, stock car, stock certificate.

#97 / CATEGORIES / PAGE 77

left: every figure is made of four straight lines; *right:* every figure is made of three straight lines.

#98 / ASSEMBLIES / PAGE 77

There are seven ways to fit the pieces into the box, as shown below. There are six ways to place the two purple L shapes. When the Ls are both along the diagonal, then green rectangles may go either vertically or horizontally.

#99 / WORD SEARCH / PAGE 78

The reward of a thing well done is to have done it. —*Ralph Waldo Emerson*

#100 / SHAPE COUNT / PAGE 79

The shape appears 36 times in the sizes and orientations shown below:

12   12   12

#101 / THREE OF A KIND / PAGE 80

Pairs. Pears, pair of glasses, pair of dice.

#102 / BY ANALOGY / PAGE 81

Letters 1, 3, and 4 of word one, plus letter 4 of word two.

SEAT + AGAR = **STAR**

OVER + ERAS = **ORES**

LOSE + ALAS = **LESS**

PAIR + TEAM = **PRIM**

#103 / ASSEMBLIES / PAGE 81

There are six ways to fit the pieces into the box, as shown. The top L can face left or right, and the bottom L can fit three different ways. $2 \times 3 = 6$.

#104 / WORD LADDER / PAGE 82

G A I N
L A I N
L A W N
L A W S
L O W S
L O S S

#105 / COVER STORY / PAGE 83

#106 / WORD SQUARE A / PAGE 84

AD	IN	SO
IS	DO	AN
NO	AS	ID

#107 / WORD SQUARE B / PAGE 85

AS	IR	ED	TO
DO	ET	IS	RA
IT	AD	OR	ES
RE	SO	AT	ID

#108 / WORD SQUARE C / PAGE 85

EN	MA	IR	SO	UT
IS	TO	NU	ME	RA
MU	RE	AS	IT	NO
AT	IN	OM	UR	ES
OR	US	ET	AN	MI

#109 / PERFECT MATCH / PAGE 86

Figures 5 and 8 match perfectly.

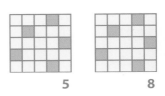

5   8

#110 / SUDOKU / PAGE 87

#111 / ASSEMBLIES / PAGE 88

There are 12 ways to fit the pieces into the box, as shown below. The dark blue piece can fit eight different places: four touching a corner and four not. When it touches a corner there are two ways to arrange the remaining pieces. When it does not touch a corner there is only

one other way to fit the remaining pieces.
$(2 \times 4) + (1 \times 4) = 12$.

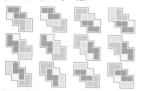

#112 / MISTRANSLATION / PAGE 88

Easy Rider. On the Waterfront. Mutiny on the Bounty. All Quiet on the Western Front. (The hints are last names of lead actors.)

#113 / CUBE SQUARED / PAGE 89

Patterns 1 and 3 look the same when folded into cubes.

#114 / PERFECT MATCH / PAGE 90

Figures 3 and 5 match perfectly.

3   5

#115 / SEEK WHENCE / PAGE 91

a. (1) (0 0) (1 1 1) (0 0 0 0) (1 1 1 1) ...
  Lengthening repetitions of 1 and 0.
b. (1 0 0 1) (1 1 1 1) (1 2 2 1)
  (1 3 . . . (1 x x 1) with increasing x.
c. (1 0 0) (1 1 1) (1 2 2) (1 3 3)
  (1 4 . . . (1 x x) with increasing x.
This puzzle is based on the research project Seek Whence (a computer program that extrapolates numerical sequences), by cognitive scientist Douglas Hofstadter, author of *Fluid Concepts and Creative Analogies*.

#116 / ASSEMBLIES / PAGE 92

There are 16 ways to fit the pieces into the box, as shown below. There are eight solutions with the dark blue piece horizontal. Mirror-reflecting those solutions gives eight more solutions with the dark blue piece vertical.

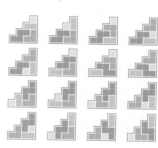

#117 / READ ME / PAGE 92

reverse engineering; backward compatible

#118 / MAZE / PAGE 93

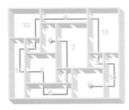

#119 / PERFECT MATCH / PAGE 94

Figures 4 and 6 match perfectly.

#120 / ALPHAMETICS / PAGE 95

9708
+ 537
10245

#121 / ASSEMBLIES / PAGE 96

There are 24 ways to fit the pieces into the box, as shown below. The four pieces can be placed in any order along the diagonal line. There are four pieces that

can be placed in the first position, three remaining pieces for the second position, two for the third position, and just one for the last position. $4 \times 3 \times 2 \times 1 = 24$.

#122 / SECRET WORD / PAGE 96

ABIDE

#123 / MENTAL BLOCKS / PAGE 97

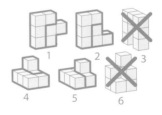

#124 / MOTION PATHS A / PAGE 98

The red point follows a curve called a cycloid that is perfectly vertical at the point where it touches the ground.

#125 / MOTION PATHS B / PAGE 99

The red point follows a straight line, while the purple point follows an elliptical path. Notice that all paths are versions of ellipses.

#126 / MOTION PATHS C / PAGE 99

The purple point swings back and forth along an arc that is slightly less than a semicircle. The red point follows a symmetrical figure-eight curve called a lemniscate.

#127 / DETAILS / PAGE 100

#128 / GRID LOGIC / PAGE 101

1 3 2
3 2 1
2 1 3

#129 / ASSEMBLIES / PAGE 101

There are 12 ways to fit the pieces into the box, as shown below. The big black square piece can be placed in any of the four corners, and the remaining pieces can always be placed three different ways. $4 \times 3 = 12$.

#130 / **CRAZY CROSS** / PAGE 102

#131 / **PAPER WORK** / PAGE 103

Arrange the six sheets in a single hexagonal loop, with each sheet overlapping the next. Two triangular loops also work.

#132 / **DETAILS** / PAGE 104

#133 / **CATEGORIES** / PAGE 105

left: every figure has one red shape; *right:* every figure has two red shapes.

#134 / **ASSEMBLIES** / PAGE 105

There are five ways to fit the pieces into the box, as shown below. The big black square piece can be placed in one of four positions. One corner doesn't allow the rest of the pieces to be placed, two corners force the rest of the pieces to be placed just one way, and the last corner allows three ways for the rest of the pieces to be placed.

#135 / **WORD SEARCH** / PAGE 106

I love deadlines. I like the whooshing sound they make as they fly by.
—*Douglas Adams*

```
E  I  E  E  D  L  T  I  D  E  R  C
O  N  M  L  E  R  O  H  S  V  E  D
E  I  O  A  E  D  A  E  H  D  L  I
T  T  N  H  E  C  G  W  B  A  E  S
I  C  L  A  P  M  T  L  I  I  I  Y
K  U  O  E  E  E  O  R  T  N  L  R
H  D  E  N  E  O  L  P  I  B  G  W
H  O  T  Y  D  O  L  E  M  C  O  O
S  R  T  H  I  U  N  E  T  G  A  S
O  P  O  U  M  N  S  D  T  H  E  L
Y  M  D  B  A  S  K  E  A  S  T  H
E  Y  F  W  A  T  E  R  L  Y  B  Y
```

#136 / LETTER PARTS / PAGE 107

6   8   4   9

2   1   5   3   7

#137 / DETAILS / PAGE 108

#138 / BY ANALOGY / PAGE 109

two consonants in word one, plus last two
letters of word two

SEA**T** + AG**AR** = **STAR**

POO**L** + PR**OD** = **PLOD**

A**CH**E + HE**AD** = **CHAD**

PO**R**E + ST**AY** = **PRAY**

#139 / ASSEMBLIES / PAGE 109

There are 15 ways to fit the pieces into
the box, as shown below. Systematically
place the upper L in every possible
position, starting from the top, then find
where the other L can go, allowing both
green pieces to fit. Only interlocking the
two Ls together at the bottom allows the
two green pieces to fit two different ways.

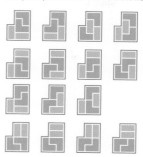

#140 / WORD LADDER / PAGE 110

L E A F
D E A F
D E A D
D E E D
F E E D
F L E D
F L E E
F R E E
T R E E

#141 / BODY SHAPES / PAGE III

This is how hands join in the middle of the knot.

#142 / MILEAGE A / PAGE 112

The next time the trip meter is the first four digits of the odometer is in 1010.1 miles, when the numbers 13355.7 and 133.5 will appear on the mileage indicators. If you are allowed to reset the trip meter, you only need to drive 124.7 miles.

#143 / MILEAGE B / PAGE 113

After 861.1 miles the numbers 13206.7 and 984.5 appear on the mileage indicators. A mere .9 miles later it happens again with the numbers 13207.6 and 985.4 appearing. If you can reset

the trip meter, then the best answer is to drive 2.2 miles, reset the trip meter, drive another 47.8 miles for a total of 50 miles, at which time the numbers 12395.6 and 047.8 will appear on the mileage indicators. You can do even better by backing up 1.4 miles, resetting, then backing up another 35.5 miles (total 36.9 miles), but the best answer is to drive forward 7.3 miles, reset, then back 12.4 miles (total 19.7 miles), giving readings of 12340.5 and 987.6.

#144 / MILEAGE C / PAGE 113

The longest distance during which the odometer never shows all 10 digits is 24,691,357.8 miles, which happens between 987,654,321.0 and 012,345,678.9 on the odometer. These two numbers are the first readings before and after all 0s on the odometer that all 10 digits appear. To prove this is the best answer, note that the odometer cannot contain all 10 digits if the first two digits are the same. The only time the first two digits roll over from one number with both digits the same to another such number is from 99 to 00. That means that for any other pair of consecutive double digit numbers, say, 39 to 40, there is at least one pair of odometer readings starting with those numbers that each contain all 10 digits, and the distance between those two readings must always be less than 20,000,000 miles.

#145 / THREE OF A KIND / PAGE 114

Bows. Rainbow, violin bow, bow and arrow.

#146 / SUDOKU / PAGE 115

4	1	6	3	2	5
2	6	5	1	3	4
3	5	2	4	1	6
5	2	3	6	4	1
6	4	1	2	5	3
1	3	4	5	6	2

1	4	5	6	3	2
2	3	1	4	6	5
5	6	2	3	4	1
6	2	4	5	1	3
3	1	6	2	5	4
4	5	3	1	2	6

#147 / CAN YOU DIGIT / PAGE 116

$$\begin{array}{r} 78 \\ + 1956 \\ \hline 2034 \end{array}$$

#148 / OUT OF ORDER / PAGE 116

near vs. far; over vs. under; all vs. nothing; closed vs. open

#149 / SHAPE COUNT / PAGE 117

The figure appears $128 + 32 + 8 + 2 = 170$ times.

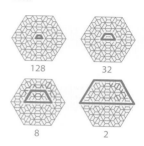

128   32

8   2

#150 / THREE OF A KIND / PAGE 118

Chinese inventions. Fireworks, kites, paper.

#151 / CATEGORIES / PAGE 119

left: Each letter has a hole in it; *right:* no hole.

#152 / CAN YOU DIGIT / PAGE 119

$$\begin{array}{r} 43 \\ + 5978 \\ \hline 6021 \end{array}$$

#153 / READ ME / PAGE 120

once in a blue moon; green with envy

#154 / COVER STORY / PAGE 121

KING MAC
LEAR BETH

#155 / FOUR OF A KIND / PAGE 122

The four alchemical elements. Earth, air, fire, water.

#156 / WHO SAT WHERE? / PAGE 123

Fay sat in seat 2. Carl sat in seat 5, the only seat directly behind another seat. Deb sat in front in seat 1. Ed sat farther forward than Barb, so Abe and Barb must be in the back row in seats 4 and 6. Ed is farther right than Carl, so he must be in the middle row in seat 3. That leaves seat 2 for Fay.

#157 / CAN YOU DIGIT / PAGE 124

```
  8 4 3
+ 7 5 9
-------
1 6 0 2
```

#158 / SECRET WORD / PAGE 124

STRUM

#159 / CUBE SQUARED / PAGE 125

Patterns 1 and 6 look the same when folded into cubes

#160 / BLOOD TYPES / PAGE 126

1. Type O− can donate to all the other blood types.
Type AB+ can receive from all the other blood types.
2. There are six possible such chains:
O− to O+ to A+ to AB+
O− to O+ to B+ to AB+
O− to A− to A+ to AB+
O− to A− to AB− to AB+
O− to B− to B+ to AB+
O− to B− to AB− to AB+

#161 / MATCHED SETS A / PAGE 127

Couples 1 and 7 have only one potential match. Couples 5, 8, 9, and 13 have the most potential matches: four.

#162 / MATCHED SETS B / PAGE 127

Here is the best possible matching, which includes all 14 couples. For more information on Optimized Match, see optimizedmatch.com.

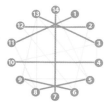

#163 / PERFECT MATCH / PAGE 128

Figures 4 and 8 match perfectly.

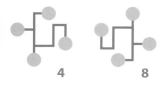

#164 / GRID LOGIC / PAGE 129

3 4 18
36 6 1
2 9 12

#165 / CAN YOU DIGIT / PAGE 129

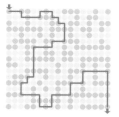

#166 / MISTRANSLATION / PAGE 130

Practice what you preach. Out of sight, out of mind. Money is the root of all evil. Still waters run deep. Never say die.

#167 / MAZE / PAGE 131

#168 / PERFECT MATCH / PAGE 132

Figures 3 and 8 match perfectly.

3   8

#169 / CATEGORIES / PAGE 133

left: red dot is in the left half of the figure; *right:* red dot is in the right half.

#170 / CAN YOU DIGIT / PAGE 133

#171 / WORD SEARCH / PAGE 134

Name me an emperor who was ever struck by a cannonball. —*Charles V*

#172 / MENTAL BLOCKS / PAGE 135

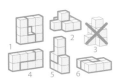

#173 / PERFECT MATCH / PAGE 136

Figures 2 and 4 match perfectly.

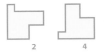

#174 / BY ANALOGY / PAGE 137

1. ABC is to ABD as XYZ is to XYA (advance last letter) or WYZ (A and Z are anchors; move letter at other end from anchor one letter away from anchor). 2. EQE is to QEQ as RVVVR is to VRRRV (reverse letters), or RRRVRRR (reverse repetitions). 3. FG is to GH as FFG is to GGH (advance letters) or FGFGH (see FFG as F-FG) or FFFGG (lengthen each string in FF-G). 4. GFF is to GGF as AAABB is to AABBB (reverse repetitions) or BBBAA (map number of repetitions onto position in alphabet) or AAAAAAAB (double the As and halve the Bs).

#175 / CAN YOU DIGIT / PAGE 137

$$9403 \times 7$$
$$65821$$

#176 / WORD LADDER / PAGE 138

There are several solutions, including:

```
FROWN    FROWN
FLOWN    FLOWN
FLOWS    FLOWS
SLOWS    SLOWS
SLOTS    SLOTS
SLITS    SPOTS
SUITS    SPITS
SUITE    SPITE
SMITE    SMITE
SMILE    SMILE
```

#177 / PAPER WORK / PAGE 139

Arrange the six sheets in two layers of triangles, one twisted atop the other as shown in the diagram. Each sheet touches its two neighbors in the same layer, plus all three sheets in the other layer.

#178 / GEOBOARDS A / PAGE 140

Constructions 1, 2, 4, and 5 are possible, but not 3 and 6.

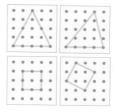

#179 / GEOBOARDS B / PAGE 141

Constructions 2, 3, 5, and 6 are possible, but not 1 and 4.

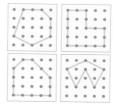

#180 / GEOBOARDS C / PAGE 141

Constructions 2, 3, 4, and 5 are possible, but not 1 and 6.

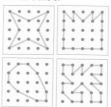

#181 / DETAILS / PAGE 142

#182 / SUDOKU / PAGE 143

①	5	6	3	2	4
6	②	4	1	3	5
4	3	⑤	2	1	6
3	4	1	⑥	5	2
2	6	3	5	④	1
5	1	2	4	6	③

②	4	5	6	1	3
1	⑥	3	2	5	4
5	3	①	4	2	6
4	5	2	③	6	1
3	1	6	5	④	2
6	2	4	1	3	⑤

#183 / CAN YOU DIGIT / PAGE 144

```
    6 8 1 9
  ×     3
  2 0 4 5 7
```

#184 / MISTRANSLATION / PAGE 144

The Sound of Music. My Fair Lady. West Side Story. Close Encounters of the Third Kind. (The hints are the names of composers and lyricists.)

#185 / LETTER PARTS / PAGE 145

4   7   3   5   8

1   6   2

#186 / DETAILS / PAGE 146

#187 / SEEK WHENCE / PAGE 147

a. (2 1) (2 2) (2 3) (2 4) (2 5) (2 6) . . .
   (2 x) with increasing x
b. (2 1 2) (2 2 3) (2 3 4) (2 4 5) . . .
   (2 x [x + 1]) with increasing x
c. (2 1 2 2) (2 3 4 4) (2 5 6 6) . . .
   (2 x [x + 1] [x + 1]) with increasing x

This puzzle is based on the research project Seek Whence (a computer program that extrapolates numerical sequences), by cognitive scientist Douglas Hofstadter, author of *Fluid Concepts and Creative Analogies*.

#188 / CAN YOU DIGIT / PAGE 148

5 8 1 7
× 6
34902

#189 / READ ME / PAGE 148

thunderstorm (TH under STORM); cover story (C over STORY)

#190 / BODY SHAPES / PAGE 149

The other person's arms become crossed.

#191 / DETAILS / PAGE 150

This satellite photograph shows spiraling vortices created by winds sweeping across Alaska's Aleutian Islands. From the NASA Landsat Project Science Office and USGS National Center for EROS.

#192 / ALPHAMETICS / PAGE 151

89562
+ 752
90314

#193 / CAN YOU DIGIT / PAGE 152

9 1 2 7
× 4
36508

#194 / SECRET WORD / PAGE 152

ABHOR

#195 / SHAPE COUNT / PAGE 153

Cubes appear 27 + 8 + 1 = 36 times.

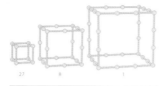

27   8   1

#196 / OLOGY-OLOGY A / PAGE 154

1. Agrology — e. Soil for crops
2. Campanology — a. Bells
3. Cetology — g. Whales
4. Cytology — c. Cells
5. Dactylology — d. Sign language
6. Dendrology — f. Trees
7. Etiology — b. Causes or origins

#197 / OLOGY-OLOGY B / PAGE 155

1. Geomorphology — b. Land forms
2. Lithology — f. Rocks
3. Meteorology — g. Weather
4. Metrology — c. Measurement
5. Mycology — e. Mushrooms
6. Myology — d. Muscles
7. Oology — a. Eggs

#198 / OLOGY-OLOGY C / PAGE 155

1. Pomology — c. Fruit
2. Rhinology — e. Nose
3. Selenology — d. Moon
4. Semiology — f. Signs
5. Speleology — a. Caves
6. Vexillology — b. Flags
7. Vulcanology — g. Volcanoes

#199 / THREE OF A KIND / PAGE 156

Words that start with the sound of PARIS.
Parasols, Paris Fance, periscope.

#200 / GRID LOGIC / PAGE 157

**S E A
U R N
B A Y**

#201 / CAN YOU DIGIT / PAGE 157

```
    3 4 5
  ×  7 8
2 6 9 1 0
```

#202 / WORD SEARCH / PAGE 158

#203 / CRAZY CROSS / PAGE 159

Alice's Adventures in Wonderland Through the Looking Glass

#204 / THREE OF A KIND / PAGE 160

Star. Stars on a flag, the star that is our sun, sea star.

#205 / CATEGORIES / PAGE 161

left: each figure contains three dots that lie on a straight line; *right:* no three dots lie on a straight line.

#206 / CAN YOU DIGIT / PAGE 161

```
    4 7
+ 2 9 6 8
  3 0 1 5
```

#207 / WORD SEARCH / PAGE 162

Housework can't kill you, but why take a chance? —*Phyllis Diller*

#208 / CUBE SQUARED / PAGE 163

Patterns 2 and 3 look the same when folded into cubes.

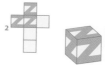

#209 / THREE OF A KIND / PAGE 164

Belt. Black belts, conveyor belt, seat belts.

#210 / BY ANALOGY / PAGE 165

Join the two words, then use letters 1, 4, 5, and the last letter.

S E A T + A G A R = STAR

H O P E + A R = HEAR

F O R + L A S T = FLAT

B Y + R I D E = BIDE

#211 / CAN YOU DIGIT / PAGE 165

$$3907 \times 4 = 15628$$

#212 / WORD LADDER / PAGE 166

B E A C H
P E A C H
P E R C H
P A R C H
M A R C H
M A R C S
M A R E S
W A R E S
W A V E S

#213 / MAZE / PAGE 167

#214 / PATTERNS A / PAGE 168

#215 / PATTERNS B / PAGE 169

#216 / PATTERNS C / PAGE 169

#217 / PERFECT MATCH / PAGE 170

Figures 2 and 8 match perfectly.

2   8

#218 / SUDOKU / PAGE 171

#219 / CAN YOU DIGIT / PAGE 172

$$9168 \times 3 = 27504$$

#220 / OUT OF ORDER / PAGE 172

blue + sky, red + tomato, green + grass, yellow + canary

#221 / MENTAL BLOCKS / PAGE 173

#222 / PERFECT MATCH / PAGE 174

Figures 1 and 8 match perfectly.

1   8

#223 / CATEGORIES / PAGE 175

left: symmetrical; *right:* asymmetrical.

#224 / CAN YOU DIGIT / PAGE 175

$$289 + 746 = 1035$$

Alternatively, the 2 and 7 in the hundreds place can be swapped.

#225 / READ ME / PAGE 176

to have and to hold (2 half and 2 holed); to be or not to be (two Bs or knot two Bs)

#226 / PAPER WORK / PAGE 177

Arrange the six sheets in a single hexagonal loop, with each sheet overlapping two sheets on either side.

#227 / PERFECT MATCH / PAGE 178
Figures 3 and 5 match perfectly.

3   5

#228 / WHO SAT WHERE? / PAGE 179
Fay sat in seat 4. If Barb sat in the red seat 1, then Abe and Carl sat in seats 3 and 5 in one order or the other. Ed sat in seat 6, just to the right of Barb. The only way Deb can sit opposite Abe is for Abe to sit in 5, with Deb in 2, leaving Carl in 3. That leaves seat 4 for Fay.

Fay

#229 / CAN YOU DIGIT / PAGE 180

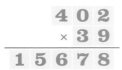

#230 / SECRET WORD / PAGE 180
LAUGH

#231 / LETTER PARTS / PAGE 181

7   4   2   8

1   3   6   5

#232 / VOTE-OLOGY A / PAGE 182
85 votes. Six states vote 6 to 5 in favor of the winner, whereas the other five states are 11 to 0 in favor of the loser.

#233 / VOTE-OLOGY B / PAGE 183
All but one state. Ten states are 6 to 5 in favor of the winner, whereas the remaining state is 11 to 0 in favor of the loser. In this case the loser receives 61 votes, and the winner receives 60. By the way, the same could theoretically happen in U.S. elections: one candidate wins 49 states each by one vote and loses the remaining state by 50 or more votes.

#234 / VOTE-OLOGY C / PAGE 183

119 of the 121 votes. There are just three states: two states with one person each who vote for the winner, and one state with 119 people, all of whom vote for the loser.

#235 / DETAILS / PAGE 184

Red-winged blackbirds. From the U.S. Fish & Wildlife Service.

#236 / BOOKSHELF / PAGE 185

The order of the books is 523614. PUSHUP (book 4) must be next to DIESEL (book 1) because no other book shares a letter with PUSHUP. The only complete order that starts with a red book is 523614.

#237 / DOT MATRIX / PAGE 185

The next figure contains 15 dots. Each successive figure adds a new column on the right containing 3 dots, then 4, 5, 6, etc.

#238 / MISTRANSLATION / PAGE 186

Strike while the iron is hot. First come, first served. The proof of the pudding is in the eating. There is more than one way to skin a cat. To err is human.

#239 / BODY SHAPES / PAGE 187

Right hands cross over; left hands cross under.

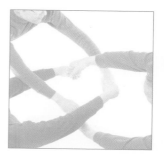

#240 / DETAILS / PAGE 188

Ornamental ceramic flowers on a pavilion of the Grand Palace, Bangkok.

#241 / CATEGORIES / PAGE 189

left: every figure has a completely enclosed area; *right:* has no completely enclosed area.

#242 / DOT MATRIX / PAGE 189

The next figure contains 37 dots. Each successive figure adds a new ring around the outside containing 6 dots, then 12, 18, 24, etc.

#243 / WORD SEARCH / PAGE 190

Take only pictures, steal only time, leave only footprints. —*Unknown*

#244 / SHAPE COUNT / PAGE 191

6 triangles (5 small + 1 big) ×
4 directions (parallel to the 4 faces of the tetrahedron) = 24 triangles

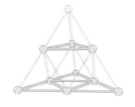

#245 / DETAILS / PAGE 192

Portion of stained glass window at Buckfast Abbey, Devon, UK.

#246 / BY ANALOGY / PAGE 193

Join the two words, then use letters 1, 3, 5, 7.

THIS + NOSE = TINS

ALSO + ERA = ASEA

TAR + HERE = TREE

SLANG + GAIN = SAGA

#247 / DOT MATRIX / PAGE 193

The next figure contains 20 dots. Two more dots complete the fifth line of the star.

#248 / WORD BUBBLES / PAGE 194

OVEN
OVERT
OVERDO
OVERAGE
OVERTURE
OVERDRIVE
OVERWHELMS
OVERANALYZE
Bonus word: MANGROVE.

This puzzle is based on the brain game Word Bubbles on Lumosity.com

#249 / COVER STORY / PAGE 195

#250 / EUCLID A / PAGE 196

Step 3: Construct a circle with center B and radius AB. Steps 4–5: Draw lines AC and BC, where C is a point where the two circles intersect.

#251 / EUCLID B / PAGE 197

Step 5: Draw a line from A to D (a point of intersection of the two big circles). This defines the point E, which is the third corner of the square. Steps 6–7: From points E and B, draw circles with radius AB. This defines point F, which is the fourth corner of the square. Steps 8–9: Draw the final two sides of the square, BF and EF.

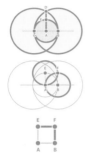

#252 / EUCLID C / PAGE 197

Step 4: Draw a circle with center C and radius CB. You now have the six corners of the regular hexagon. Steps 5–10: Draw the six sides of the hexagon.

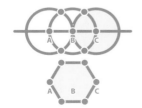

#253 / THREE OF A KIND / PAGE 198

Fire starters. Magnifying glass, matches, lightning.

#254 / SUDOKU / PAGE 199

4	3	1	6	5	2
5	6	2	4	1	3
1	2	3	5	4	6
2	5	6	1	3	4
6	4	5	3	2	1
3	1	4	2	6	5

6	1	2	3	4	5
4	3	5	6	2	1
2	5	1	4	6	3
5	4	3	2	1	6
3	6	4	1	5	2
1	2	6	5	3	4

#255 / DOT MATRIX / PAGE 200

The next figure contains 45 dots. The cross is made of five squares, whose sides grow by one each step. The squares have 1 dot, then 4, 9, 16, etc.

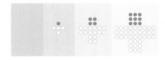

#256 / MISTRANSLATION / PAGE 200

The Grapes of Wrath. Singing in the Rain. Gone with the Wind. Some Like It Hot. (The hints are the names of the directors.)

#257 / CUBE SQUARED / PAGE 201

Patterns 2 and 4 look the same when folded into cubes.

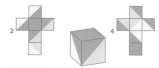

#258 / THREE OF A KIND / PAGE 202

Diamond: King, queen, and jack of diamonds; baseball diamond; diamond ring.

#259 / SEEK WHENCE / PAGE 203

a. (1 2) (2 3) (3 4) (4 5) (5 6) (6 7) (7 8) (8 . . .(x [x+1]) with increasing x

b. (1) (2 2) (3 3) (4 4 4) (5 5 5) (6 6 6 6) . . . Repeated x with increasing x, where the number of repetitions of x within each parenthetical group is taken from the sequence itself

c. (1) (2 2) (3 3) (4) (5) (6 6) (7 7) (8) (9) (10 10) . . . Repeated x with increasing x, where the number of repetitions is the sequence (1 2) (2 1) (1 2) . . .

#260 / DOT MATRIX / PAGE 204

The next figure contains 32 dots. At each step a new side is added to the square. Completing the last side adds only four dots, not eight.

#261 / READ ME / PAGE 204

floating a loan; kitchen sink.

#262 / MAZE / PAGE 205

Alternative solution: The left most vertical line can move one column to the right.

#263 / THREE OF A KIND / PAGE 206

Things that flip over. Pancakes, gymnast, hourglass.

#264 / ALPHAMETICS / PAGE 207

```
   98775
+105703
 204478
```

#265 / DOT MATRIX / PAGE 208

The next figure contains 24 dots. The two squares have 32 dots. The top square moves down and to the left one dot at each step. The area of overlap removes 0, 3, 8, 9 . . . dots.

#266 / SECRET WORD / PAGE 208

IMBUE

#267 / MENTAL BLOCKS / PAGE 209

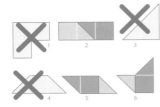

#268 / GIBBERISH A / PAGE 210

1. Mixed metaphor
2. Productive error
3. Spoonerism
4. Malapropism
5. Greasy spoonerism
6. Cannibalism
7. Malaphor

#269 / GIBBERISH B / PAGE 211

1. Shun sign = sunshine
2. Coarse mode = Morse code
3. Fair oil = airfoil
4. Lead of spite = speed of light
5. Lumber nine = number line
6. Mentor of sass = center of mass
7. Tech wrangle = rectangle
8. Toe preen = protein
9. Walk shave = shockwave
10. Wine save = sine wave

#270 / GIBBERISH C / PAGE 211

1. How to recognize speech using common sense.
2. Humpty Dumpty sat on a wall.
3. Little Red Riding Hood. Once upon a time, there was a little girl who lived with her mother in her little cottage, on the edge of a large dark forest.

#271 / PERFECT MATCH / PAGE 212

Figures 3 and 5 match perfectly.

3

5

#272 / BOOKSHELF / PAGE 213

The order of the books is 624135. ABACUS (book 6) must be the first book because no other title has A as the second letter. That forces BRAKES (book 2) to be next, and so on.

#273 / DOT MATRIX / PAGE 213

The next figure contains 25 dots. At each step a new ring of dots is added around the outside. The new rings have 4 dots, then 8, 12, 16, etc.

#274 / CRAZY CROSS / PAGE 214

#275 / PAPER WORK / PAGE 215

Overlap three sheets in a triangle, then add three more sheets at the corners, as shown below.

#276 / PERFECT MATCH / PAGE 216

Figures 1 and 6 match perfectly.

#277 / CATEGORIES / PAGE 217

left: every figure has two black squares of the same size; *right:* every figure has two black squares of different sizes.

#278 / DOT MATRIX / PAGE 217

The next figure contains 27 dots. At each step a new arm is added to the spiral to fill out a rectangular outline. The figure grows by 5 dots, then 6, 7, 8, etc.

#279 / WORD SEARCH / PAGE 218

Virtue has its own reward, but no box office. —Mae West

#280 / LETTER PARTS / PAGE 219

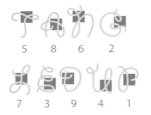

5 8 6 2

7 3 9 4 1

#281 / PERFECT MATCH / PAGE 220

Figures 1 and 8 match perfectly.

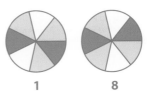

1 8

#282 / BY ANALOGY / PAGE 221

Move letter 1 of first word to end; ignore second word.

TEAS + SEAT = **EAST**

EROS + ROES = **ROSE**

SNAP + SPAN = **NAPS**

STAR + ARTS = **TARS**

#283 / DOT MATRIX / PAGE 221

The next figure contains 16 dots. The number of dots keeps increasing by four.

#284 / WORD BUBBLES / PAGE 222

COME
COMMA
COMBAT
COMBINE

COMEDIAN
COMMANDER
COMPROMISE
COMMUNICATE
Bonus word: INTERCOM.
This puzzle is based on the brain game
Word Bubbles on Lumosity.com

#285 / BODY SHAPES / PAGE 223

If any one person withdraws from the
assembly, the other two people will no
longer be linked.

#286 / HARRY POTTER A / PAGE 224

The F bottle must be in either position 3
or 4. The eight arrangements are:

P W F P P W B
P W P F P W B
B P W F P P W
B P W P F P W
P P W B F P W
P P W F B P W
B P P W F P W
B P F P W P W

#287 / HARRY POTTER B / PAGE 225

The smallest bottle must be in either
position 3 or 4. The biggest bottle must
be in either position 2 or 6, in order to
eliminate possible solutions that have
poison in both positions 2 and 6.

#288 / HARRY POTTER C / PAGE 225

1. The only safe bottle in all possible
arrangements that meet all the other
conditions is bottle 7.
2. In this case there are two possible
orders: BPPWFPW and BPWFPPW. In either
case Hermione could safely choose bottle
1 as B. Not knowing whether bottle 4 or 5
was F, the best she could do would be to
give bottle 4 to Harry to drink. If it proved
to be wine, which would not protect him
from the forward fire, he could then
drink bottle 5, knowing it was F. But that
would work only if there was a way to
distinguish W and F without dying.

#289 / DETAILS / PAGE 226

#290 / SUDOKU / PAGE 227

#291 / DOT MATRIX / PAGE 228

The final frame contains 18 dots. From one frame to the next, the first column gets one more dot, the second column gets two more dots, and the third column loses one dot.

#292 / OUT OF ORDER / PAGE 228

dog + bark, cat + meow, snake + hiss, donkey + bray.

#293 / SHAPE COUNT / PAGE 229

Each of the five monochromatic quadrilaterals contains four individual triangles and four triangles made up of two adjacent triangles. Plus there are 13 triangles encircling the central triangular hole, including the hole itself, and two long triangles down the right stroke of the A. 20 + 20 + 13 + 2 = 55 triangles total.

#294 / DETAILS / PAGE 230

#295 / CATEGORIES / PAGE 231

left: left edge is a tall vertical line; *right:* left edge is not a tall vertical line.

#296 / DOT MATRIX / PAGE 231

The final frame contains 11 dots. From one frame to the next, the two vertical arms of the figure move together.

#297 / READ ME / PAGE 232

big bang; it's a small world after all

#298 / MAZE / PAGE 233

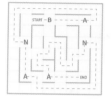

#299 / DETAILS / PAGE 234

#300 / WHO SAT WHERE? / PAGE 235

Fay sat in seat 5. The only place Ed could sit that is farther forward than three other people is seat 1. That means that the couples Abe and Barb, and Carl and Deb, sat in seats 2 and 4, and 3 and 6. That leaves seat 5 for Fay.

#301 / DOT MATRIX / PAGE 236

The final frame contains 13 dots. From one frame to the next, the diamond continues to move to the right, intersecting the vertical line in three dots in the fourth frame.

#302 / SECRET WORD / PAGE 236

BAWDY

#303 / MENTAL BLOCKS / PAGE 237

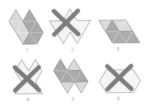

#304 / SHAPE UP A / PAGE 238

The spaces for seeds are in fivefold pentagonal symmetry. The apple flower also has pentagonal symmetry.

#305 / SHAPE UP B / PAGE 239

Tying a strip of paper in an overhand knot and flattening it creates a regular pentagon.

#306 / SHAPE UP C / PAGE 239

Slicing a cube of cheese in half this way reveals a regular hexagon.

#307 / THREE OF A KIND / PAGE 240

Jack. Jack-in-the-box, car jack, game of jacks.

#308 / BOOKSHELF / PAGE 241

The order of the books is: 214635. HALT (book 2) can only be next to BEND (book 1). From there on the rest of the order is forced: BEND must then also be next to MASK (book 4), and so on.

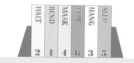

#309 / SPARE CHANGE / PAGE 241

The largest amount of postage you cannot make exactly with 4- and 7-cent stamps is 17 cents. You can make 18 cents as 4 + 7 + 7, 19 cents as 4 + 4 + 4 + 7, 20 cents as 4 + 4 + 4 + 4 + 4, and 21 cents as 7 + 7 + 7. From there on just add more 4-cent stamps to make every amount of postage above 21 cents.

#310 / MISTRANSLATION / PAGE 242

Behind the eight ball. Asleep at the switch. The short end of the stick. Penny-wise and pound-foolish.

#311 / LETTER PARTS / PAGE 243

#312 / THREE OF A KIND / PAGE 244

Scale. Fish scales, balance scales, scale model.

#313 / CATEGORIES / PAGE 245

left: red dot is counterclockwise from where the tail joins the body; *right:* red dot is clockwise.

#314 / SPARE CHANGE / PAGE 245

You can make exact change for 50 cents using 10 coins as 5 pennies, 4 nickels, and 1 quarter; or as 5 pennies, 1 nickel, and 4 dimes; or as 10 nickels.

#315 / WORD SEARCH / PAGE 246

Many go fishing without knowing it is fish they are after. —*Henry David Thoreau*

#316 / BODY SHAPES / PAGE 247

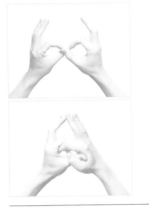

#317 / THREE OF A KIND / PAGE 248

Tie. Tie-dye, necktie, musical tie symbol.

#318 / BY ANALOGY / PAGE 249

Join the two words, delete first two and last two letters, reverse the others.

T**IED** + **IT**EM = **TIDE**

C**UP** + **U**RN = **UP**

SH**OW** + **T**OW = **TWO**

US**E** + **MAG**IC = **GAME**

#319 / SPARE CHANGE / PAGE 249

The most change you can have is $1.19, made up of three quarters, four dimes, and four pennies.

#320 / WORD BUBBLES / PAGE 250

CARE
CARVE
CARPET
CARDIAC
CAROUSEL
CARTWHEEL
CARBONATED
CARNIVOROUS
CARBOHYDRATE
Bonus word: STREETCAR

#321 / SHAPE COUNT / PAGE 251

The numbers in the big figure indicate how many pentagons use that particular concave angle. The small figures show all the pentagons at four of the angles. 3 + (3 + 1 + 1 + 2) + (3 + 1 + 1 + 2) = 17 pentagons total.

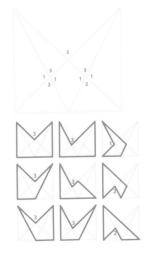

#322 / COMBO CAFÉ A / PAGE 252

1. There are six possible combination plates: three different plates with all items the same color, and three different plates with all items the same shape.

2. There are 27 possible combination plates. If, for example, you start with a yellow item, you then have a choice of three different red shapes for the second and three different green shapes for the third ($3 \times 3 \times 3 = 27$).

#323 / COMBO CAFÉ B / PAGE 253

1. There 84 possible different combinations. For the first item you can choose any one of nine items. Because all items on the plate must be different, that leaves eight choices for the second item and seven for the third, for a total of 504 combinations ($9 \times 8 \times 7 = 504$). But 504 is not the final answer. Here's why. The order of items in a combination doesn't matter; ABC, ACB, BAC, BCA, CAB, and CBA all count as the same combination. That means we have counted every combination six times instead of just once. So we divide 504 by 6 and get the final answer 84.

2. There are 81 possible combination plates. The only combinations excluded are those that have only one shape. There are three such combinations, each containing all three colors of a single shape. That leaves 81 combinations ($84 - 3$).

#324 / COMBO CAFÉ C / PAGE 253

1. There are 36 possible combination plates. There are three possible color pairings and three possible shape pairings, for a total of nine (3×3) possible combinations of two colors and two shapes. For each such combination there are four possible items to choose from (two colors and two shapes), and there are just four ways to choose three items from a set of four. So the total number of combination plates is $9 \times 4 = 36$.

2. There are six possible combination plates. For the first color you have three choices of shape. For the second color there are two remaining choices of shape. For the third and last color you must choose the one leftover shape ($3 \times 2 \times 1 = 6$).

#325 / PERFECT MATCH / PAGE 254

Figures 2 and 4 match perfectly.

2

4

#326 / SUDOKU / PAGE 255

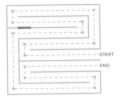

#327 / SPARE CHANGE / PAGE 256

The largest amount of postage you cannot make exactly with 5- and 8-cent stamps is 27 cents. You can make 28 cents as 5 + 5 + 5 + 5 + 8, 29 cents as 5 + 8 + 8 + 8, 30 cents as 5 + 5 + 5 + 5 + 5 + 5, 31 cents as 5 + 5 + 5 + 8 + 8, 32 cents as 8 + 8 + 8 + 8. From there on just add more 5-cent stamps to make every amount of postage above 32 cents.

#328 / MISTRANSLATION / PAGE 256

Top Gun. True Lies. Catch Me If You Can. Raiders of the Lost Ark.

#329 / MAZE / PAGE 257

#330 / PERFECT MATCH / PAGE 258

Figures 1 and 3 match perfectly.

#331 / SEEK WHENCE / PAGE 259

a. (1 1) 2 (3 3) 5 (5 5) 8 (7 7) 11 (9 9) 14 . . . Alternate between two sequences: two copies of an ascending odd number: (1 1) (3 3) (5 5), and an ascending sequence going up by three: 2 5 8 11 14.

b. (1 1) (2 3) (3 5) (4 7) (5 9) (6 11) (7 13) (8 . . . Alternate between two sequences: counts in ascending order 1, 2, 3, 4, 5, 6, 7, 8, and an ascending sequence going up by two: 1, 3, 5, 7, 9, 11, 13.

c. (1 1) 2 (3 3) 5 (7 7) 10 (13 13) 17 (21 21) . . . Keep repeating three operations: doubled number, +n, +n.
On the first cycle n = 1. On the second cycle n = 2, and so on.

This puzzle is based on the research project Seek Whence (a computer program

that extrapolates numerical sequences), by cognitive scientist Douglas Hofstadter, author of *Fluid Concepts and Creative Analogies*.

#332 / SPARE CHANGE / PAGE 260

You can make exact change for 30 cents using six coins as six nickels, or as five pennies and one quarter.

#333 / READ ME / PAGE 260

circular reasoning; cross-examination

#334 / MENTAL BLOCKS / PAGE 261

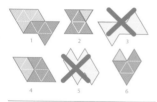

#335 / PERFECT MATCH / PAGE 262

Figures 1 and 7 match perfectly.

#336 / ALPHAMETICS / PAGE 263

```
    9856
+1396873
 1406729
```

#337 / SPARE CHANGE / PAGE 264

The most change you can have is $143, made up of 4 twos, 1 five, 4 twenties, and 1 fifty.

#338 / SECRET WORD / PAGE 264

HOIST

#339 / LETTER PARTS / PAGE 265

#340 / DNA MAZE A / PAGE 266

#341 / DNA MAZE B / PAGE 267

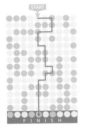

#342 / DNA MAZE C / PAGE 267

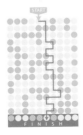

#343 / DETAILS / PAGE 268

#344 / BOOKSHELF / PAGE 269

The order of the books is: 652134. Book 6 (Five) must come first because it is not the title of any other book. From there on the order is forced.

#345 / SPARE CHANGE / PAGE 269

The smallest possible total value of the money in each hand is 40 cents, which equals four dimes, or three nickels and one quarter.

#346 / CRAZY CROSS / PAGE 270

#347 / BODY SHAPES / PAGE 271

Thumb touches thumb and forefinger touches forefinger.

ALTERNATE ANSWER:
Left thumb touches right forefinger; left forefinger and right thumb reach through to touch in back. Knot faces away from you.

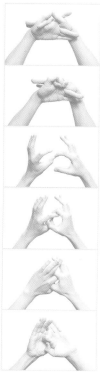

#348 / DETAILS / PAGE 272

#349 / CATEGORIES / PAGE 273

left: every figure has an axis of mirror symmetry; *right:* no figure has an axis of mirror symmetry.

#350 / SPARE CHANGE / PAGE 274

The most change you can have is $1.63, made up of four two-cent coins, four twenty-cent coins, and three quarters, or one quarter and one 50-cent piece.

#351 / SHAPE COUNT / PAGE 274

The numbers indicate how many L shapes there are of each size. Some of the mid-sized L shapes are hard to see because they cross color boundaries.
16 + 4 + 4 + 1 + 1 = 26 L shapes total.

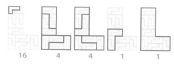

#352 / WORD SEARCH / PAGE 275

Never go to bed mad. Stay up and fight.
—*Phyllis Diller*

#353 / DETAILS / PAGE 276

Pinball machine.

#354 / BY ANALOGY / PAGE 277

Starting with first letter of first word, substitute next letter in alphabet for every other letter.

RISE + DOOR = **STEP**

CANE + DIRT = **DOES**

SITE + FORT = **TUGS**

PITY + HUSK = **QUIT**

#355 / SPARE CHANGE / PAGE 277

The largest amount of postage you cannot make exactly with 7- and 11-cent stamps is 59 cents. You can make 60 cents as $7 + 7 + 7 + 7 + 7 + 7 + 7 + 11$, 61 cents as $7 + 7 + 7 + 7 + 11 + 11 + 11$, 62 cents as $7 + 11 + 11 + 11 + 11 + 11$, 63 cents as $7 + 7 + 7 + 7 + 7 + 7 + 7 + 7 + 7$, 64 cents as $7 + 7 + 7 + 7 + 7 + 11 + 11$, 65 cents as $7 + 7 + 11 + 11 + 11 + 11$, and 66 cents as $11 + 11 + 11 + 11 + 11 + 11$. From there on just add more 7-cent stamps to make every amount of postage above 59 cents.

#356 / WORD BUBBLES / PAGE 278

INCITE
INCOME
INCHING
INCISOR
INCUBATE
INCENTIVE
INCENDIARY
INCONGRUOUS
INCANDESCENT
Bonus word: INCOGNITO.

This puzzle is based on the brain game Word Bubbles on Lumosity.com.

#357 / MAZE / PAGE 279

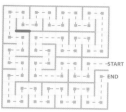

#358 / GEO SCRAMBLE A / PAGE 280

1. parallelogram
2. hyperbola
3. tetrahedron
4. trigonometry

#359 / GEO SCRAMBLE B / PAGE 281

1. polyhedra
2. perpendicular
3. perimeter
4. diameter

#360 / GEO SCRAMBLE C / PAGE 281

1. equilateral
2. isosceles
3. bisector
4. hypotenuse

#361 / THREE OF A KIND / PAGE 282

Dolly. Hand truck dolly, child's dolly, Salvador Dalí.

#362 / SUDOKU / PAGE 283

5	4	1	3	6	2
2	5	3	4	1	6
6	2	5	4	1	3
3	6	2	5	4	1
1	3	6	2	5	4
4	1	3	6	2	5

1	4	2	5	3	6
2	3	6	1	5	4
4	6	3	2	1	5
3	5	1	6	4	2
6	1	5	4	2	3
5	2	4	3	6	1

#363 / SPARE CHANGE / PAGE 284

If you have lots of 3-cent coins and nothing else, there is no limit to the amount of change you can have and not be able to make exact change for a dollar.

#364 / OUT OF ORDER / PAGE 284

aunt + uncle, son + daughter, brother + sister, father + mother

#365 / MENTAL BLOCKS / PAGE 285

#366 / **THREE OF A KIND** / PAGE 286

Shuttle. Shuttlecock, shuttle for a loom, space shuttle.

#367 / **CATEGORIES** / PAGE 287

left: each letter has a horizontal stroke; *right:* no horizontal stroke.

#368 / **SPARE CHANGE** / PAGE 287

The smallest possible total value of the money in each hand is 45 cents, which equals nine nickels, or five pennies and four dimes.

#369 / **READ ME** / PAGE 288

middle of the road; edge of insanity

#370 / **LETTER PARTS** / PAGE 289

#371 / **THREE OF A KIND** / PAGE 290

Eight. Eight-sided gazebo, figure-eight knot, eight-armed octopus.

#372 / **WHO SAT WHERE?** / PAGE 291

Fay sat in seat 6. There are just two ways to pair up the six seats in diagonal pairs: 14—26—35 and 16—42—35. The only way Abe can be just in front of Ed and Barb can also be to the left of someone else is for Abe to be in seat 1 and Barb in seat 4, which puts Ed in seat 2, and therefore Fay in seat 6.

#373 / **SPARE CHANGE** / PAGE 292

The smallest possible total value of the money in each hand is 80 cents, which equals eight dimes, or five pennies and three quarters.

#374 / **SECRET WORD** / PAGE 292

WOULD

#375 / **BODY SHAPES** / PAGE 293

Actually, mirrors can reverse top and bottom—just stand on a mirror that lies flat on the floor. We say that mirrors reverse left and right because most mirrors are mounted vertically, and we refer to the two symmetrical halves of our body as left and right.

#376 / SLICE IT UP A / PAGE 294

There are 6 + 6 + 2 = 14 different ways to dissect a hexagon into isosceles triangles, using only noncrossing diagonals. The three basic dissections are shown below, along with the number of ways you can rotate or flip each figure. This puzzle was inspired by a problem in the movie *Hard Problems* (hardproblemsmovie.com), which documents the American team of high school students competing in the International Math Olympiad.

6   6   2

#377 / SLICE IT UP B / PAGE 295

Here are ways to dissect the hexagon and octagon into isosceles triangles, using only noncrossing diagonals.

#378 / SLICE IT UP C / PAGE 295

Shown is a dissection of the 12-gon into isosceles triangles, using only noncrossing diagonals. Notice that you can create this dissection by starting with the dissected hexagon above and adding a skinny isosceles triangle "peak" to each side of the hexagon dissection (doubling the number of sides). To

produce a similar dissection for the 24-gon, add a skinny isosceles triangle "peak" to each side of the 12-gon dissection. For the 48-gon, add peaks to the 24-gon. For the 64-gon, add peaks to the octagon dissection; for the 80-gon, add peaks to the pentagon dissection.

#379 / PERFECT MATCH / PAGE 296

Figures 1 and 7 match perfectly.

1   7

#380 / BOOKSHELF / PAGE 297

The order of the books is: 456312. The last book must be BOO because it shares a letter with only the one book, BAT. Working backward, BAT must be preceded by CANDY, then SPIDER, SKULL, and SCREAM.

#381 / PATHOLOGY / PAGE 297

There are eight different paths. There are two roads from one dot to the next, and three chances to make a choice. $2 \times 2 \times 2 = 8$ paths.

#382 / MISTRANSLATION / PAGE 298

Call a spade a spade. Make no bones about it. Cast pearls before swine. What goes around comes around.

#383 / SQUARE COUNT / PAGE 299

$9 + 3 + 20 + 9 + 2 = 43$ squares

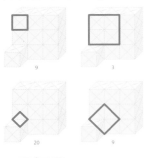

9

3

20

9

2

#384 / PERFECT MATCH / PAGE 300

Figures 2 and 6 match perfectly.

2   6

#385 / CATEGORIES / PAGE 301

left: no figure contains a right angle; *right:* every figure contains a right angle.

#386 / GO FIGURE / PAGE 302

The smallest possible sum is 10. You get the smallest sum when the ages are close together. The closest ages that multiply to 36 are 3, 3 and 4, which add to 10.

#387 / MAZE / PAGE 302

#388 / **WORD SEARCH** / PAGE 303

Great spirits have always encountered violent opposition from mediocre minds.
—*Albert Einstein*

```
P R O P O S A L G R E A
T T S P Y I R I T S E C
H S H A V C E A L W L A
Y K I G S E N N C O P O
U C E N I N T E C E M R
E A V D T E V K D E A F
I T I O L U W E R N X A
N T D T O I I U P P E C
O A E S S I T T I O T
N F N E R L O M I M E U
D I C O U C R E M V I A
N D E C N A L A B S E L
```

#389 / **PERFECT MATCH** / PAGE 304

Figures 3 and 8 match perfectly.

3   8

#390 / **BY ANALOGY** / PAGE 305

letters 1, 2, and 4 of second word, plus letter 1 of first word

T**EAS** + **EAT**S = **EAST**

E**VEN** + **RO**E**S** = **ROSE**

T**EN** + **TE**E**N** = **TENT**

D**UAL** + **KIL**N = **KIND**

#391 / **PATHOLOGY** / PAGE 305

There are 24 different paths. 2 choices × 3 choices × 4 choices = 24 paths. 12 paths start with the high road, and 12 start with the low road.

#392 / **WORD BUBBLES** / PAGE 306

REST
RESET
RESCUE
RESTATE
RESIDENT
RESERVOIR
RESTAURANT
RESUSCITATE
RESERVATIONS
Bonus word: TREASURES

This puzzle is based on the brain game Word Bubbles on Lumosity.com.

#393 / **MENTAL BLOCKS** / PAGE 307

#394 / **CHAIR GAME A** / PAGE 308

1. 24 weeks. Imagine seating the four people in order, one at a time. The first person has a choice of four chairs. That leaves the second person with a choice of three chairs, for a total of $4 \times 3 = 12$ combinations so far. The last two people can sit in the remaining two chairs in two different ways, so the total number is $4 \times 3 \times 2 = 24$ combinations.

2. Six clinks. Each pair of people must clink glasses, and there are six pairs of people among four people (AB, AC, AD, BC, BD, and CD).

#395 / **CHAIR GAME B** / PAGE 309

1. Eight weeks. The north and south chairs can be occupied by either the Whites or the Blacks with the other couple in the east and west chairs (two combinations), and for each of those combinations each couple can be in one of two orders (four combinations). Altogether, $2 \times 4 = 8$ combinations.

2. 16 weeks. There are 24 combinations allowing anyone to sit anywhere. Remove the eight combinations in which members

of each couple are sitting opposite each other and you are left with the combinations in which members of each couple sit side by side.

#396 / **CHAIR GAME C** / PAGE 309

1. 48 weeks. There are three pairs of opposite seats, which can be assigned to the three couples six different ways. Within each pair of opposite seats the two members of a couple can be seated two different ways. Six couple patterns times eight ($2 \times 2 \times 2$) ways to switch members of all couples = 48 combinations.

2. 96 weeks (12 couple patterns times eight ways to switch members of all couples). There are two ways to group the six seats as three adjacent pairs. Each grouping of three adjacent pairs can be assigned to the three couples 6 different ways. Within each pair of opposite seats the two members of a couple can be seated two different ways. Two groupings times six couple patterns times eight ($2 \times 2 \times 2$) ways to switch members of all couples = 96 combinations.

#397 / **DETAILS** / PAGE 310

#398 / SUDOKU / PAGE 311

#399 / PATHOLOGY / PAGE 312

There are five different paths. At each dot you can go straight or diagonal.

#400 / MISTRANSLATION / PAGE 312

Back to the Future. The Matrix Reloaded. Spiderman. Minority Report.

#401 / BODY SHAPES / PAGE 313

#402 / DETAILS / PAGE 314

#403 / SEEK WHENCE / PAGE 315

a. (1 2 1) (2 3 2) (3 4 3) (4 5 4) (5 6 5)
(6 . . .)
(x x + 1 x) with increasing x.
b. (1 2) (1 2) (3 2) (3 2) (5 2) (5 2)
(7 2) (7 2) . . .
(x 2) with x equal to increasing odd
numbers, and each pair repeated twice.
c. 1 (2) 1 (2 3 2) 1 (2 3 4 3 2) 1
(2 3 4 . . .)
A series of mountains of increasing
length. First mountain starts from 1,
counts up to 2, then back down to 1.
Second mountain climbs one higher to 3.
And so on.

This puzzle is based on the research
project Seek Whence (a computer program
that extrapolates numerical sequences),
by cognitive scientist Douglas Hofstadter,
author of *Fluid Concepts and Creative
Analogies*.

#404 / PATHOLOGY / PAGE 316

There are six different paths. Each path
uses a different combination of two
vertical roads. 1 + 2 + 3 = 6 paths.

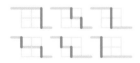

#405 / READ ME / PAGE 316

running joke; standing offer

#406 / SHAPE COUNT / PAGE 317

17 + 4 + 1 + 4 + 1 = 27 squares

#407 / DETAILS / PAGE 318

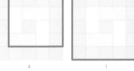

#408 / ALPHAMETICS / PAGE 319

```
  59778
+   634
-------
  60412
```

#409 / PATHOLOGY / PAGE 320

There are 11 different paths. Nine paths travel only left to right, and two include at least one right-to-left road. 9 + 2 = 11 paths.

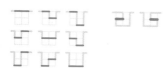

#410 / SECRET WORD / PAGE 320

INEPT

#411 / MAZE / PAGE 321

Alternative solution: The path from N to END can go over instead of under the single vertical wall.

#412 / PENTOMINOES A / PAGE 322

Play the dark piece shown. The game is over because the only pieces that fit in the narrow corridor of space remaining on the board are the pieces already on the board.

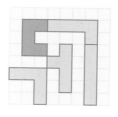

#413 / PENTOMINOES B / PAGE 323

Here are two ways to put three pentominoes on a 6 × 6 board so no more pentominoes can be placed. The two solutions use completely different pieces. In the four-piece for the 7 × 7 board, no piece touches the edge of the board.

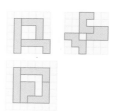

#414 / PENTOMINOES C / PAGE 323

Here are ways to place six pieces on a
9 × 9 board, and seven pieces on a
10 × 10 board, so no more pieces can
be placed. These solutions work because
there are six different pentominoes that
cannot be squeezed into a strip that is
only two squares wide.

#415 / THREE OF A KIND / PAGE 324

Spiral shape. Snail shell, spiral staircase,
spiral notebook.

#416 / BOOKSHELF / PAGE 325

The order of the books is: 315462.
COM must come first because nothing
can precede it. From there on the order
is forced.

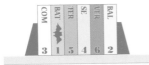

#417 / PATHOLOGY / PAGE 325

There are 11 different paths. Four paths
stay in the upper half, four stay in the
lower half, one goes through the middle,
and two zigzag between upper and lower
halves. 4 + 4 + 1 + 2 = 11 paths.

#418 / CRAZY CROSS / PAGE 326

#419 / MENTAL BLOCKS / PAGE 327

#420 / THREE OF A KIND / PAGE 328

Grand. Grand piano, Grand Canyon, grandfather clock.

#421 / CATEGORIES / PAGE 329

left: the diagonals slope downhill to the right; *right:* the diagonals slope uphill to the right.

#422 / PATHOLOGY / PAGE 329

There are 36 different paths. There are six paths through the left half of the map, and six through the right half of the map, for a total of 6 × 6 = 36 complete paths.

#423 / WORD SEARCH / PAGE 330

Worries go down better with soup than without. —*Jewish Proverb*

#424 / BODY SHAPES / PAGE 331

Here are three of the many possible three-hand handshakes.

#425 / THREE OF A KIND / PAGE 332

Oil. Oil lamp, oil wells, french fries fried in oil.

#426 / BY ANALOGY / PAGE 333

1. ABC is to ABD as XYZ is to XYA (advance last letter) or WYZ (A and Z are anchors; move letter opposite anchor away from anchor).
2. AABC is to AABD as IJKK is to IJLL (advance final letters) or HJKK (move letter opposite the doubled letter away from doubled letter).
3. ABC is to ABD as MRRJJJ is to MRRKKK (advance last letter) or MRRJJJJ (increase number of repetitions).
4. EFG is to DFG as GHI is to FHI (retreat first letter) or GHJ (move letter at opposite end from G away from G).

#427 / PATHOLOGY / PAGE 333

There are 21 different paths. Of the paths that travel only left to right, four paths stay in the upper half, four stay in the lower half, one goes through the middle, and two zigzag between upper and lower halves.

Of the paths that include at least one right-to-left road, six include one of the first two diagonals, and four more include one of the last two diagonals. 4 + 4 + 1 + 2 + 6 + 4 = 21 paths.

#428 / WORD BUBBLES / PAGE 334

ALLOT
ALLUDE
ALLEGRO
ALLUVIAL
ALLIANCE
ALLEGEDLY
ALLNIGHTER
ALLEGIANCES
ALLITERATION
Bonus word: REINSTALL

This puzzle is based on the brain game Word Bubbles on Lumosity.com.

#429 / SHAPE COUNT / PAGE 335

54 + 16 + 4 + 2 + 2 = 78 squares.

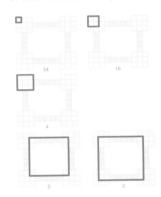

#430 / LIP READING A / PAGE 336

1. THINK
2. SHIP
3. UNDER

#431 / LIP READING B / PAGE 337

1. CHOICE
2. AGREE
3. SINGLE

#432 / LIP READING C / PAGE 337

1. ASPECT
2. AFRAID
3. PROVEN

#433 / PERFECT MATCH / PAGE 338

Figures 2 and 8 match perfectly.

2   8

#434 / ALPHAMETICS / PAGE 339

$$520068$$
$$+968286$$
$$1488354$$

#435 / PATHOLOGY / PAGE 340

There are 15 different paths. Each path uses a different combination of two vertical roads. $1 + 2 + 3 + 4 + 5 = 15$ paths.

#436 / OUT OF ORDER / PAGE 340

car + driver, horse + rider, book + reader, computer + user

#437 / MAZE / PAGE 341

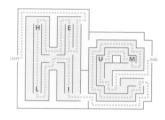

#438 / PERFECT MATCH / PAGE 342

Figures 1 and 4 match perfectly.

1   4

#439 / ALPHAMETICS / PAGE 343

$$95823$$
$$+91823$$
$$187646$$

#440 / PATHOLOGY / PAGE 344

There are 13 different paths. At each dot you can go straight or diagonal. Five paths start straight, five start with two diagonals, and three start with a diagonal and a straight. 5 + 5 + 3 = 13 paths.

#441 / READ ME / PAGE 344

forty days and forty nights; foreign legion

#442 / MENTAL BLOCKS / PAGE 345

#443 / PERFECT MATCH / PAGE 346

Figures 3 and 6 match perfectly.

#444 / ALPHAMETICS / PAGE 347

```
  3 4 0 3 2
+ 9 1 4 4 6
─────────
1 2 5 4 7 8
```

#445 / PATHOLOGY / PAGE 348

There are 12 different paths. Nine paths travel only left to right, and three include at least one right-to-left road. 9 + 3 = 12 paths

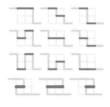

#446 / SECRET WORD / PAGE 348

CLOWN

#447 / BODY SHAPES / PAGE 349

#448 / MONOLITHS A / PAGE 350

#449 / MONOLITHS B / PAGE 351

#450 / MONOLITHS C / PAGE 351

Here are ways to cut a solid hexahedron into five tetrahedra (one entirely inside and four on the surface), and a solid tetrahedron into four nonrectangular hexahedra.

#451 / PATTERNS A / PAGE 352

The shapes are in alphabetical order, based on the letter each shape looks like: F-I-L-P-N-T-U-V-W-X-Y-Z. Some of the shapes need to be turned diagonally to look like their letters.

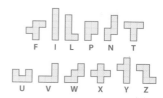

#452 / PATTERNS B / PAGE 353

The three shapes, reading right to left, spell the word SHALOM in Hebrew.

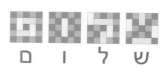

ש   ל   ו   ם

#453 / PATTERNS C / PAGE 354

This diagram is a map of this book, with a square for every puzzle. The colors correspond to the puzzle genres: green = visual, blue = logic, orange = number, pink = word, and teal = spatial.

ACKNOWLEDGMENTS

I'd like to thank my editor, Megan Nicolay, for the idea for this book, Ariana Abud for designing a beautiful and engaging layout, and all of their colleagues at Workman for working so hard to make this book a reality. And to my readers of *Discover Magazine, Games, Newmedia,* and my annual *Amazing Mind Benders* Page-A-Day® calendar—thank you for your loyalty and interest over the years. If you have any comments or questions, I'd love to hear from you.

ABOUT THE AUTHOR

SCOTT KIM is a game and puzzle designer with a background in graphic design, mathematics, music, and computer science. Since 1990, he has created thousands of puzzles for books, electronic games, toys, and magazines like *Discover, Games,* and *Scientific American.* A true puzzle master, with a BA in Music and a PhD in Computers and Graphic Design from Stanford University, Scott seeks to create thought-provoking experiences with a sense of wonder and insight. He is the author of *Inversions* (Key Curriculum Press), *The Playful Brain* (with Richard Restak, Riverhead Books), and nine years of the *Amazing Mind Benders* Page-A-Day® calendar (Workman). He is now designing games for mathematics education.